MASTERGATE

AND

POWER FAILURE

MASTERGATE

AND

POWER FAILURE

2 Political Satires for the Stage

LARRY GELBART

APPLAUSE
NEW YORK • LONDON

AN APPLAUSE ORIGINAL

MASTERGATE AND POWER FAILURE:
Two Political Satires for the Stage
By Larry Gelbart

Library of Congress Cataloging-in-Publication Data

Gelbart, Larry.
   Mastergate and power failure : 2 political satires for the stage / by Larry Gelbart.
     p.   cm.
   ISBN 1-55783-177-7
   1. Political satire, American. 2. Political plays, American.
I. Title.
PS3557 .E368A6   1994
812' .52--dc20   94-1204
                                            CIP

British Library Cataloging-in-Publication Data

A catalogue record of this book is available from the British Library

APPLAUSE BOOKS

211 W. 71ST STREET, NEW YORK, NY 10023
PHONE: 212-595-4735 FAX: 212-721-2856

406 VALE ROAD, TONBRIDGE KENT TN9 1XR
PHONE: 0732 357755 FAX: 0732 770219

FIRST APPLAUSE PRINTING: 1994

CONTENTS

MASTERGATE

A Play on Words

Mastergate was originally produced by the American Repertory Theatre, Cambridge, Massachusetts, and was presented by Gene Wolsk at the Criterion Center Stage Right, New York City, on October 12, 1989, with the following cast:

The Committee:

Senator Bowman, The Chairman ....Jerome Kilty
Congressman Proctor ....Tom McDermott
Shepherd Hunter, Chief Counsel for the
    Committee ....John Dossett
Congressman Byers ....Wayne Knight
Senator Bunting ....Jeff Weiss
Congressman Sellers..Jeff Weiss
Senator Knight ....Wayne Knight

The Witnesses:

Steward Butler ....Wayne Knight
Abel Lamb ....Steve Hofvendahl
Major Manley Battle ....Daniel von Bargen
Secretary of State Bishop ....Tom McDermott
Vice President Burden ....Joseph Daly
Wylie Slaughter ....Jeff Weiss

The Lawyers

Mr. Child, Mr. Picker, Mr. Boyle, Mr. Carver.............Zach Grenier

For Total Network News:

Merry Chase ....Melinda Mullins
Clay Fielder ....Joseph Daly
TNN Director ....Katrina Stevens
TNN Cameramen................Merrill Holtzman, Harold Dean James

The Wives

Mrs. Butler, Mrs. Lamb, Mrs. Battle, Mrs. Burden,
    Mrs. Slaughter ....Ann McDonough
Pages....................Charles Geyer, Isiah Whitlock, Jr., Priscilla C. Shanks
Secret Service Man ....William Cain

Directed by Michael Engler
Scenery by Philipp Jung
Costumes by Candice Donnelly
Lighting by Steven Strawbridge
Sound by Mark Salzberg
Video by Dennis Diamond

The time is the morning after.

The place is Washington, D.C.

The action is relentless, with no intermission.

Onstage, an empty Hearing Room. As the audience finds its seats, the Pages constantly enter and exit, bringing in and placing large loose-leaf binders, pencils, legal tablets, water pitchers, drinking glasses and name-plates for the Committee Members (some of whom are mannequins), all done at a brisk pace. As a newsperson, serious, sensuous MERRY CHASE, *appears in the anchor area, Committee Members, Staffers and Aides, other Reporters and Spectators enter, take their places, creating a hum of activity and anticipation. Every Committee Member, every Witness, with one exception, wears a blue suit and a red, patterned tie. When(ever)* MERRY CHASE *addresses the TNN cameras, all others go on about their business. The pictures taken by the cameramen are seen on various TV monitors placed about the theatre.*

MERRY CHASE [*To camera, after making sure her hair is just right*]: This is Merry Chase, Total Network News, speaking to you from the Sherman Adams Room in the John Mitchell Building in Washington, D.C., on this, the first morning of our gavel-to-gavel coverage of the long-awaited start of the opening session of the House Select Committee to Investigate Alleged Covert Arms Assistance to Alleged Other Americas. Given that these

11

promise to be lengthy hearings, the Joint Committee can probably use all the excessiveness at its command since — [*Seeing that the* Committee Members *have taken their places*] let's go over to the Chairman, who is about to —

> *The Chairman,* SENATOR BOWMAN, *takes his place next to elderly* CONGRESSMAN PROCTOR. BOWMAN *raps his gavel.*

Here is Senator Bowman.

> BOWMAN *continues to gavel the room to order.*

BOWMAN [*Overlapping* MERRY CHASE's *last sentence*]: Can we have it quiet, please? I'd like to get started on time, if we can, inasmuch as we're late already. Thank you. Thank you very much. Even though a few of the Members of the Committee have not been able to get away from a roll call vote on the floor of the House, I'm advised that since enough of us are not all there, we can go ahead with these hearings here. I would like, if I may, to begin by presenting a preamble I've prepared for the purpose of broadly narrowing down the scope of what these hearings hope to accomplish. [*Reads*] "If we, as a nation, have learned anything from Water and Iran-Contragates, it is that those who forget the past are certain to be subpoenaed. Hence, the formation of this Permanent Select Joint Committee, which I share the co-privilege of occupying the chair of with my distinguished colleague, one of my oldest and longest friends, the Honorable Oral Proctor, of the House of Representatives, and which was charged some ten months ago by the President of the United States with conducting an exhausting inquiry into the most recent example of debilitating governmental self-abuse, which has become known throughout the media as 'Mastergate.' This panel, which intends to give every appearance of being bipartisan, will be ever-mindful of the President's instructions to dig as far down as we can, no matter how high up that might take us. Let me emphaticize one thing at the outset. This is not a witch hunt. It is not a trial. We are not looking for hides to skin, nor goats to scape. We're just trying to get all the facts together in one room at the same time in the hope that they'll somehow recognize one another. Our chief goal, of course is to answer the question: 'What did the President know, and does he have any idea that he knew it?'" The Committee will call its first witness Mr. Steward Butler.

> *A burst of flashbulbs, as* BUTLER *goes to the witness table, accompanied by his lawyer,* CHILD. MRS. BUTLER *takes the seat all the wives will occupy. During this:*

MERRY CHASE [*To camera*]: Steward Butler was a key player in the earliest phases of the Mastergate affair. A young man once thought to have a very bright future in government, he has since enjoyed an almost meteoric disappearance. He is currently handling blanket appeals for the Bureau of Indian Affairs.

BOWMAN: Mr. Butler, do you swear that the testimony you are about to give is the truth, the whole truth and nothing but the truth?

Before BUTLER *can speak:*

CHILD: He does.

BOWMAN [*Annoyed*]: *He* has to.

BUTLER: Then, I do, too, sir.

BOWMAN: Will the witness please state his name for the record?

CHILD: His name is Steward Butler, sir.

BOWMAN: And you yourself are who, sir?

CHILD: My name is Foster Child, Mr. Chairman. I am with the law firm of Prior, Pastor, Priest and Pope.

BOWMAN: Mr. Child, I'll ask you to remember, sir, that Mr. Butler is the witness, not a conduit. We're not pressing his button so we can hear you ring.

CHILD: Just doing my job, sir.

BOWMAN: Fine. Let's not start in on overtime.

CHILD: Yes, sir.

BOWMAN: Thank you. Mr. Hunter, are you ready to begin the questioning?

HUNTER: Yes, sir.

BOWMAN: You may start to begin then, if you would.

HUNTER: Thank you, Mr. Chairman. Good morning, Mr. Butler.

> BUTLER *looks to* CHILD, *who nods his approval to answer.*

BUTLER [*To* HUNTER]: Good morning, sir.

MERRY CHASE [*To camera*]: This is Shepherd Hunter, the Chief General Counsel for the Combined Permanent Select Committees.

HUNTER [*Overlapping*]: Mr. Butler, as you know, I am Chief General Counsel for the Combined Permanent Select Committees, and in that role you and I have spent many hours in earlier, preliminary hearings, in which you were interrogated by Staff Members of the Members of this Committee, and later sub-questioned by Sub-staff Members of this Permanent Committee's Temporary Sub-Committee.

BUTLER: I believe I know that, yes, sir.

HUNTER: None of my questions, therefore, should come as any great surprise.

BUTLER: No, sir.

HUNTER: Nor any of your answers.

BUTLER: We can only hope.

HUNTER: Mr. Butler, you were, during the period in time in question, employed by the Department of Justice?

BUTLER: Yes, sir.

HUNTER: Would I also be correct in saying that that position which you held is one you no longer do?

BUTLER: Yes, you would, in that, no, I don't.

HUNTER: You were dismissed by the Justice Department?

BUTLER: I am on a permanent leave of absence, yes, sir.

HUNTER: You were fired, is that what you're saying?

BUTLER: It's my guess that I am, yes, sir.

HUNTER: And can you tell us, prior to that occurrence, what your title was, sir, during the series of past events, the accumulative effect of which led up to the present time?

BUTLER: I was, for the purpose of your answer, acting as Assistant to the Acting Assistant Deputy Attorney General.

HUNTER: In respect to that capacity, I would ask you to please direct your remarks to the meeting that took place in the Assistant Attorney General's office on February 25th of last year.

BUTLER: The year preceding this one chronologically?

HUNTER: The one immediately before.

BUTLER: Meetings have a way of blurring together, Mr. Hunter. We tended to meet every time we got together.

HUNTER: For the purpose of specificity, I refer you to Page Two-Eighty-five of Binder "B," Section Seven, Sub-paragraph six, big "A," little "d," which contains your name listed as being among one of those who participated in that particular meeting.

BUTLER: I see my name, yes, sir.

HUNTER: We can therefore assume you attended.

BUTLER: Not necessarily, sir.

HUNTER: Mr. Butler, either you did or you didn't.

BUTLER: Or else I didn't, though I did.

CHILD: Mr. Hunter, if I can perhaps help to avoid a respondatorial redundancy; although Mr. Butler's name does, without question, appear in the meeting's minutes, he did not, in fact, spend one minute in the meeting.

HUNTER: Mr. Butler, can you tell the Committee how you happened to be there inasmuch as you weren't?

BUTLER: Yes, sir. Due to the ongoing upheavalment at

Justice during that period, a great many of us in the Department had to be in a great many different places, often at the same time. I was unable to attend the meeting that took place during the period of your question since I had been assigned to overlook the work of Assistant Attorney General Cleaver, who suddenly found himself out of the loop during that particular time frame.

HUNTER: On the day of the meeting.

BUTLER: If that's what I said, yes.

HUNTER: Doing what exactly was the Assistant Attorney General doing, can you tell us?

BUTLER: I believe I'm about to, yes, sir. Mr. Cleaver was giving testimony that day.

HUNTER: And the Assistant Attorney General was giving testimony regarding what exactly was he?

CHILD: Mr. Chairman, I believe that answer is classified.

HUNTER: The answer has appeared in the nation's press, Mr. Chairman.

BOWMAN: If you're concerned, Mr. Child, I can assure you that this Committee can keep a secret, once it's been on the six o'clock news.

CHILD: Thank you, Mr. Chairman.

BOWMAN: Now that we've dealt with the question of the question, can we try to get an answer to it, as well?

HUNTER: The Assistant Attorney was giving testimony regarding what, Mr. Butler?

BUTLER: Regarding the Special Prosecutor's efforts to indict the Acting Attorney General for conflict of interest in pardoning the former Attorney General, who was convicted of conspiracy charges that he had inadvertently filed against himself, but which later proved to be quite damaging.

HUNTER: Returning to the meeting of the 25th . . .

BUTLER: Yes, sir.

HUNTER: The one you did not attend.

BUTLER: Along with the others.

HUNTER: Who did.

BUTLER: Who didn't. There was mostly no one there who actually was.

HUNTER: But you do know who the subject of the meeting was, do you not?

BUTLER: I do.

HUNTER: The subject of the meeting was Mr. Victor Gamble, was it not?

BUTLER [*Getting the okay from* CHILD]: It was.

HUNTER: I would like you, if you would, to walk us through that talk, Mr. Butler, zooming in in particular on Victor Gamble, the man himself, sir. He is an international financier, is he not? With financial interests on an international scale?

BUTLER: That is the spectrum of his range, yes, sir. Not surprising, since, while Mr. Gamble was originally born an American, he only spends depreciable amounts of time in this country, preferring to operate out of Liechtenstein through an off-shore Libyan corporation, which is based in the Bahamas, while, for purposes of domicility, he resides in Switzerland in a consecutive series of unnumbered houses.

HUNTER: He is, for all intensive purposes, a tax fugitive?

BUTLER: That is my conviction, sir, based on several of his own.

HUNTER: Can you tell the Committee how much money Victor Gamble owes the United States government presently at this time? It's pretty well up in nosebleed country, is it not?

BUTLER: To the best of what I've heard, yes, sir.

HUNTER: Two hundred million dollars, is it not?

BUTLER: That's ballpark enough, yes, sir.

HUNTER: These would be back taxes?

BUTLER: Plus interest on those and other similar arrears he's behind on, plus fines, penalties and court costs on his previous convictions for fraud, evasion, attempted bribery of Federal officials and several counts of perjury.

HUNTER: And Mr. Gamble, has, more or less, put himself beyond the reach of the law of the land?

BUTLER: He has not been in the United States since the Chamber of Commerce voted him "Man of the Year."

HUNTER: There have been efforts made to make Mr. Gamble make good?

BUTLER: In March of last year, the same year in which the previous February occurred, Mr. Gamble was ordered to comply with a federal court order ordering him to surrender certain audits and financial statements. Since his compliance was of the non-variety, we then obtained a second court order ordering that for every day Mr. Gamble withheld what the first court order ordered, he would be fined on the order of one hundred thousand dollars.

HUNTER: A hundred thousand dollars per day.

BUTLER: I know it takes some government people weeks to make that kind of money, sir, but since Mr. Gamble holds, among others, a Colombian passport, he was able to take advantage of the fact that, in that country, a criminal fine is deductible as an operating expense.

HUNTER: And so his response was?

BUTLER: Nil to none, sir. When the tab reached eight million three, the penny finally dropped that Mr. Gamble was not only not going to surrender his records, but that he was also going to stonewall us on the penalty payments and that it was time to take some positive steps.

HUNTER: Please tell the Committee what these steps were which you undertook to take.

BUTLER: Yes, sir. Considering that Mr. Gamble's diversification of interests range from mills to malls, with holdings in everything from aero to office space, the decision decided upon was to confiscate one of Mr. Gamble's holdings to pay a portion, or any part thereof, of what he owed the US Government.

HUNTER: Which choice became what?

BUTLER: Well, given its pick of all of Mr. Gamble's various "goodies," as we called them, the Government's best optionary move seemed to be the takeover of MPI.

HUNTER: MPI being Master Pictures, Incorporated, the motion picture studio owned by Victor Gamble?

BUTLER: Yes, sir. Master Pictures, Incorporated.

HUNTER: Can you thumbnail for the members of this Committee a brief history of MPI — Master Pictures, Incorporated, please?

BUTLER: Yes, sir. [*A long drink of water, then*] Master Pictures was formed in 1925 on the lower East side of New York City by an immigrant from pre-Russian Latvia, a furniture upholsterer named Max Stern. When one of his clients defaulted payment on an order of folding chairs, Mr. Stern repossessed the chairs and the store in which they were located, which, as it turned out, happened to be one of the early movie houses. After taking over the operation, it wasn't long before Mr. Stern realized that, while you could only make a profit on a chair once, you could sell the viewing of a movie over and over and over, and that, no matter how many times you sold somebody the opportunity to see it, the movie still belonged to you. With that understanding, it was only a matter of time before Mr. Stern started turning out what his patrons were looking at, instead of sitting on. In the following three years, Mr. Stern shot over three hundred silent films in the back of his shop, taking the tacks out of his upholsterer's mouths and having them act during their lunch hours. In 1928, Mr. Stern moved the company to California to facilitate his twin goals in life — the making of the cheapest possible movies and getting as far away from the Czar as possible. Although he soon built Master Pictures into one of the most successful studios in Hollywood, it all came tumbling down when Mr. Stern refused to convert his facilities following the invention of sound. His feeling was that after a day at work or an evening at home, no one in their right mind would pay to hear someone else talk. Mr. Stern, who had lived like a king, died a broken, penniless man, who was cremated with a borrowed match. The studio was rocked by a power struggle, eastern banks and Western unions, but eventually the reins were wrested away under the control of Mr. Stern's son-in-law, Mr. Miles Walker, a telent agent, who, over the years, had married three out of four of Mr. Stern's daughters. MPI returned to its former glory under a board of directors consisting of five of his sons, four of whom were also first cousins. The studio achieved so great a degree of financial success that it eventually caught the eye of several corporate raiders, chief among them, Mr. Victor Gamble. Though Gamble gained control of MPI by means of an LBO, he admittedly knew nothing about the process of making and marketing motion pictures. Given this advantage, he doubled the company's profits in one year. In time, he neglected the studio altogether, and the profits tripled. The opinion therefore arrived at here in Washington was that if the IRS could maintain the studio's high level of incompetence, MPI might prove just as financally rewarding to the US government. [*He takes another long drink*]

HUNTER: Thank you, Mr. Butler.

BUTLER: Thank you, sir.

HUNTER: I have no use for the witness at this time, Mr. Chairman.

BOWMAN: Thank you, Mr. Hunter. Mr. Proctor? Do you wish to interrogate the witness, sir?

PROCTOR: Thank you, Mr. Chairman, just briefly I do, yes. I don't intend to take up any more time than I will.

MERRY CHASE [*To camera*]: Congressman Oral Proctor; as sharp today as he was when he entered the House thirty terms ago.

BOWMAN: My learned colleague rarely does.

PROCTOR: I just have one or two questions which I don't quite understand. Mr. Butler.

BUTLER: Sir?

PROCTOR: Was it the consensus of this idea, the crux of your thrust, that by taking over a movie company, our Government would become active in the production of motion pictures in the same manner as, shall we say, a certain Soviet Union of the USSR?

BUTLER: Sir, as I have repeatedly reiterated, the Master Pictures takeover was prompted by Mr. Gamble being in very deep yogurt with various of the Federal branches. The game plan, as I understood the broad strokes, was to separate out all of MPI's different assets and for the Government to benefit from the sale of all of them. If I may reference you, sir, to Binder "J," Schedule "K," Folder "B," the heading of which reads, "MPI Inventory." If you'll track with me, you will see the above-mentioned assets listed thereunder, the first item being the MPI library: over two hundred thousand feature films, the guesstimated value of which is in the region of the neighborhood of between thirty and forty million dollars.

PROCTOR: Yet out of all of the items listed herein, the Government has gotten rid of a total of none?

BUTLER: Not any more than that, no, sir.

PROCTOR: The real estate the studio stands on? Some three hundred and sixty prime Southern California acres, thought to be sitting atop major oil deposits or, from a housing prospective, land considered to be highly condominiable? None of it sold?

BUTLER: No, sir.

PROCTOR: In other words, although the powers that were had zeroed in on one course of action, they then promptly did a three-sixty and did something completely other.

After CHILD *jots a reply for* BUTLER.

BUTLER: Sir, with all due respect, and in my deepest opinion, because of all the confusion and chaos at the time of this period, it was decided modus vivendively-wise, to bump the entire MPI business out of our Department, with the understanding that the matter would no longer have anything whatsoever to do with Justice.

PROCTOR: By order of whom then was this matter passed on?

BUTLER [*Feeling cornered*]: I don't know for a fact, sir. I only heard it said as hearsay.

PROCTOR: Mr. Butler, having admitted denying that you voted at meetings which you did not attend, it ill-behooves you to withhold information from this Committee, some of whom hold you in enough contempt as it is. Now, whose name did you exactly hear?

BUTLER: [*Softly*]: It was Mr. Slaughter, sir.

PROCTOR: I beg your pardon?

BUTLER [*Louder, uncomfortably*]: It was Mr. Slaughter, sir.

PROCTOR: Mr. Wylie Slaughter? The Director of the CIA?

BUTLER: Yes, sir.

CROWD [*Overlapping*]: Wylie Slaughter!
Wow!
It figures.
Slaughter strikes again.
We should have known.

BOWMAN [*Gavels for order*]: Mr. Proctor.

PROCTOR: Mr. Butler, please elucidate us in your inferral regarding Mr. Slaughter's involvement, if you will.

BUTLER: I'm not saying there was any involvement

involved, sir. It's only that I just heard Mr. Slaughter's name come up at at a meeting at which I might not ever have been at the time.

PROCTOR [*Frustrated*]: Well, I have no further questions, if you have no further answers, sir. Mr. Chairman, I'm afraid I know as much as I can. I will yield whatever balance I may have left.

BOWMAN: Thank you, Mr. Proctor.

PROCTOR: Thank you, Mr. Chairman.

BOWMAN: Mr. Butler, on behalf of the Committee, I want to thank you for your largely cooperative appearance this morning. We are especially grateful, knowing how time consuming it is for you at the present time, being uncooperative as you are with the House Ethics Committee, where you are currently charged with influence peddling and obstructing justice.

BUTLER: Thank you, Mr. Chairman.

BOWMAN: The Committee will stand in recess for ten minutes and resume again in one hour.

> As the CROWD *engages in small talk and a great deal of coming and going:* MERRY CHASE, CLAY FIELDER *at her side, each with a hand mike and the obligatory finger in one ear, addresses a nearby camera.*

MERRY CHASE: And so, the Committee has rolled up its

sleeves and waded right in, laying, if not the blame, then certainly the responsibility for the start of Mastergate squarely at the feet of the former head of the CIA, Mr. Wiley Slaughter. With me now, for Total Network News, is old Washington hand, Clay Fielder. Clay, you've covered Watergate, Iran-Contra, the Agnew mess, the McCarthy hearings, the Pentagon payoffs, the Nofziger and Deaver trials, the HUD and S and L scandals; Tower, Meese, Wright, Wedtech, Bork, Bitberg. Have we, were you to opinionate, finally struck the absolute rock bottom of the barrel with the CIA takeover of a Hollywood studio, sleaze-wise speaking? Will the President be implicated, despite his denial yesterday at his yearly press conference? And what about the totally surprising but wholly unexpected revelation that Wiley Slaughter's name has surfaced as one more finger in the puzzle? In 20 seconds, your reactions so far, Clay: in just the way you see them.[*Before* FIELDER *can reply,* BOWMAN's *gavel is heard.*] Thank you, Clay, and now, it's back to the Hearing Room and Senator Bowman.

> BOWMAN *gavels the room to order.* LAMB, *the next witness, helps the pregnant* MRS. LAMB *to her seat.* LAMB's *lawyer,* PICKER, *appears.*

BOWMAN: The witness will raise his right hand, please. [LAMB *complies. Barely audible:*] You swear the testimony you are about to give is the truth, the whole truth and nothing but the truth?

MERRY CHASE [*Overlapping, to camera*]: Abel Lamb has been in government service for eight years and testifying for nine.

LAMB *and* PICKER *have taken their seats.*

PICKER: Mr. Chairman, the witness would like to say something before he says anything at all, sir.

BOWMAN: The witness will first be sworn and then we'll have a name for the record.

PICKER: Following that, I would hope he will be permitted.

BOWMAN: Anything that follows will come after. Does the witness so swear?

LAMB: I do.

BOWMAN: The I in your case being?

LAMB: My name is Abel Lamb, Mr. Chairman.

PICKER: If Mr. Lamb could read his brief statement at this time, Senator?

BOWMAN: Counsel will identify himself to the Committee.

PICKER: My name is Nat Picker, Mr. Chairman. With the Manhattan law firm of Block, Stahl, Wild and Wilder.

BOWMAN: The Committee will hear your statement,

Mr. Lamb.

LAMB: Thank you, Mr. Chairman.

BOWMAN: We will take Mr. Picker's word for it that it is a brief one, remembering that brevity is in the ear of the beholder.

LAMB: Yes, sir. Thank you. [*Reads from a prepared text*] "I wish, first of all, to extend my extreme gratitude to the Committee for the privilege of being subpoenaed, so that I might clarify the version I have given of the events under investigation. I secondly thank the Committee for granting me limited immunity, in that it gives me leeway to tell everything I know without having to tell *everything* I know. It has been most difficult remaining silent during all I've said up to now, but in lieu of the fact that certain prior actions by others, which could conceivably include myself, have been labeled as possible criminal behavior in high places, I have felt it my duty to remain steadfastly evasive and selectively honest so as to protect the national interest and, above all, to safeguard the President's security. Looking back in hindsight, there are many things I would have done differently in the past, but that I did whatever I have been told it's possible for me to say that I did because I felt I was doing my best acting in the interests of our government. I also ask the Committee to remember that, ethics and morality aside, I felt I had a higher obligation to do as I was ordered to. I'm aware that that's not an alibi, but I know you'll agree that it *is* an excuse." Thank you, Mr. Chairman.

BOWMAN: Thank you, Mr. Lamb. Mr. Hunter?

PICKER [*To* BOWMAN]: Mr. Lamb also has a closing statement he'd like to make, sir.

BOWMAN: Let's see if we can't just squeeze a few questions in between statements, shall we? Mr. Hunter?

HUNTER: Mr. Lamb.

LAMB: Mr. Hunter.

HUNTER: You are employed by the IRS, sir?

LAMB: I am.

HUNTER: The Internal Revenue Service?

LAMB: That IRS, yes, sir.

HUNTER: Would you fill the Committee in by way of your professional background, Mr. Lamb.

LAMB: Yes, sir. I was first employed by the Delaware accounting firm of Partridge and Crowe, where I was appointed executor of the then-Secretary of the Treasury Crowe's blind trust, a responsibility I held right up until the time of the Secretary's trial. Following his sentencing, and Mr. Partridge's appointment to replace him, I came on board with the IRS, where I have served for the last four years while Mr. Crowe has been serving his five-to-ten.

HUNTER: One of which years you spent on assignment in Hollywood, California, is that not correct?

LAMB: It is more correct than not, yes, sir.

HUNTER: Please tell the Committee how it is that it happened that you found yourself chosen to be picked for this particular assignment.

LAMB: Yes, sir. I would venture to surmise that under ordinary circumstances, the person who would have been more normal to select for the job would have been my immediate superior, Mr. Haggard Plowman.

HUNTER: Would that be Mr. Plowman, who was in charge of the Tax Fraud Division?

LAMB: Yes, sir. As it was, I got the nod because of Mr. Plowman having a very full plate at the time.

HUNTER: Preparing his defense in his own tax fraud case, was he not?

LAMB: Was, yes, sir. Although, I think it's only fair to add that Mr. Plowman was eventually found innocent of all the charges that were brought against him.

HUNTER: He was, nevertheless, sentenced to serve two years.

LAMB: If we're counting for contempt, yes, sir.

HUNTER: I'd like to get back to Hollywood, if I can.

LAMB: Yes, sir.

HUNTER: Upon acceptance of your assignment, what precisely did you expect your duties in California out there were to entail?

LAMB: I assumed that liquidating all of MPI's assets would be the sum of my entire entailment.

HUNTER: Can you tell the Committee how it happened that not one of the inventoried items belonging to MPI was ever, nor to the present day, in fact, has still not ever been, liquidated?

LAMB: There was a change in the game plan. If you think of the initial meeting of February 25th as our scrimmage, then the Government's plan to sell off the various parts of MPI can be seen as a decision to punt. But instead of punting, I was sent out to California. For a long pass, so to speak, this switch in tactics occurring — [*Consulting binder*] when I was summoned to a second, smaller meeting on the night following the day of the first, previous meeting.

HUNTER: And how many people who were present were at that meeting?

LAMB: If you include me, there were two.

HUNTER: There was one other person.

LAMB: Beside the one me, yes, sir.

HUNTER: You and someone else.

LAMB: I got the figure by crunching the two numbers, sir.

HUNTER: And in the person of whom would that other person have been?

LAMB: We're speaking of names?

HUNTER: With any luck at all.

LAMB: The other person was Mr. Slaughter, sir.

HUNTER: Mr. Wylie Slaughter.

LAMB: That Mr. Slaughter, yes, sir.

HUNTER: The former Director of the CIA.

LAMB: Yes, sir. But this was prior to his becoming the former.

HUNTER: I understand. Tell me, Mr. Lamb, you must have been somewhat surprised to receive an invitation from the then-Director of the CIA, were you not?

LAMB: Somewhat and then some, yes, sir.

HUNTER: Had you ever imagined that Mr. Slaughter was even aware of your existence?

LAMB: Only to the extent that Mr. Slaughter is aware of

everyone in Washington's existence.

HUNTER: And yet, here he was inviting you, a considerably low-echelon player —

LAMB: The lowest, yes, sir.

HUNTER: Inviting you to meet with him.

LAMB: No, sir.

HUNTER: You just said that he did.

LAMB: He did, sir. But not to a meeting.

HUNTER: To a discussion, then.

LAMB: A non-discussion, to be perfectly accurate, sir.

HUNTER: A non-discussion.

LAMB: Yes, sir.

HUNTER: Can you explain the distinction?

LAMB: Sir, a non-discussion is one in which the participants agree that though they are, in reality, having a discussion, for the purpose of future and probable deniability, they will maintain that no discussion, in point of fact, ever took place. Such an agreement must, of course, be non-discussed beforehand.

HUNTER: For the record, Mr. Lamb, would you say

that what you and I have been having is a discussion?

LAMB: Only if we both agree that in the future we will say that what is taking place, actually did; and therefore, what is happening really is. Otherwise, strictly speaking, we never spoke.

HUNTER: Thank you.

LAMB: Gladly, sir.

HUNTER: Mr. Lamb, can you tell us in what manner you received Mr. Slaughter's invitation to this discussion, non-or-otherwise, that took place? Did it come through routine Government channels?

LAMB: Somewhat other, sir.

HUNTER: What sort of other would that have been?

LAMB: I got it from a waiter. In a restaurant, at the end of a meal.

HUNTER: Was it on official stationery of any kind?

LAMB: Not actually, no.

HUNTER: Actually on what then was it?

LAMB: It was in a fortune cookie.

CROWD [*Laughter, overlapping*]: A fortune cookie? Real high tech stuff, huh?

Did he say a fortune cookie?
Watch *that* stock go up!

HUNTER: Inside a fortune cookie, Mr. Lamb?

LAMB: Yes, sir.

HUNTER: Just rolled up in there?

LAMB: Folded in half.

HUNTER: And it was just assumed that you would open it?

LAMB: The waiter leaned down and said, "The fortune cookies are especially good tonight, sir."

HUNTER: That must have struck you as somewhat unusual. A message of that importance, inside a fortune cookie.

LAMB: And being in an Italian restaurant at the time. Actually I *had* intended going to a Chinese restaurant that night. My wife and I only changed our mind at the last minute.

HUNTER: And you told Mr. Slaughter of this change of plans?

LAMB: At this time in time I had never either spoken to nor with Mr. Slaughter.

HUNTER: And yet he knew where you were going to

be?

LAMB: Mr. Slaughter knows things about people, sometimes even before they know them themselves, if, in fact, they ever do, should Mr. Slaughter feel that it would be best if they never did.

HUNTER: This meeting of the 26th, the one that never took place, took place where?

LAMB: At Mr. Slaughter's bedside.

HUNTER: At the time that you didn't see each other, Mr. Slaughter was in the Bethesda Naval Hospital?

LAMB: He was.

HUNTER: He was a patient there?

LAMB: He was in a gown, lying in a bed. That's what came up on my screen.

HUNTER: According to TV and press reports of that period, he had checked in ostensively to undergo a series of routine medical tests.

LAMB: I was led to misunderstand that, as well, yes, sir.

HUNTER: Mr. Slaughter was, as has since been confirmed by official denials, recovering from a heart transplant, was he not?

LAMB: His third.

HUNTER: Third transplant.

LAMB: The first two were rejected. The doctors offered the opinion that Mr. Slaughter's system seemed to resist having a heart for more than twenty-four hours at a time.

HUNTER: Can you describe Mr. Slaughter's condition upon non-seeing him at the time of your visit to the hospital?

LAMB: Yes, sir. The minute I walked into his room, I was grateful in a way that I wasn't really there. Mr. Slaughter's face was horribly twisted, only not in the way we usually know it. He was in a tremendous amount of pain, but his orders were that he be given no drugs, preferring unbearable suffering to losing control, or having anyone tap into that portion of his brain that was for his eyes only.

HUNTER: Did he — ?

LAMB [*Cuts in*]: Also, there was his lifelong fear of any drug which might have caused him to ever tell the truth during a conversation.

HUNTER: Was he coherent when you spoke?

LAMB: I understood everything he said, once I heard it.

HUNTER: Hearing him talk was a problem?

LAMB: In a manner of speaking.

HUNTER: Why was that? Did he have trouble projecting? Was he weak?

LAMB: Mr. Slaughter was hooked up to a number of life support systems, one of which caused every word he said to be delayed by several seconds, allowing an auxiliary device to instantly scan his memory bank, a copy of which was stored at the CIA, to be certain that whatever he uttered could be cleared for communication.

HUNTER: So that you didn't actually hear him at the moment he spoke?

LAMB: Not at that precise moment, no, sir. There would be short bursts of Muzak in between. "I've Got the World on a String," "Syncopated Clock," that sort of thing.

HUNTER: I'm most curious now as to the substance of what actually was said, that in preliminary testimony you've stated you recall remembering, Mr. Lamb.

BOWMAN: I'm sorry Mr. Hunter, I'm afraid I wasn't watching the time, all of which of yours has been used.

HUNTER: Thank you, Mr. Chairman.

BOWMAN: Thank you, Mr. Hunter.

HUNTER: Thank you, Mr. Lamb.

LAMB: Thank you, Mr. Hunter.

BOWMAN: Congressman Byers, I expect you would like to ask the witness some questions of your own?

BYERS: Thank you, Mr. Chairman. Mr. Lamb.

LAMB: Congressman.

BYERS: Mr. Lamb . . .

MERRY CHASE [*To camera*]: Congressman Byers, a two-termer from New Jersey, on a rare visit to Washington between international junkets to investigate the wasting of government funds.

BYERS: I'm curious now as to the substance of the content of what actually was said during your non-meeting with Mr. Slaughter, that in preliminary testimony you've stated you recall remembering.

LAMB: Yes, sir. I just hope I remember it the same way I remembered it before. First off the bat, I was informed by Mr. Slaughter that, as of that moment forward, I was to act solely upon his orders.

BYERS: His orders only? The director of the CIA told you in an ICU that you would no longer be answerable to the IRS?

LAMB: Yes, sir.

BYERS: He said that he had the power to control anyone in an appointed or elected position? That they were to ignore all previous oaths? To be loyal only to him?

LAMB: Yes, sir, he did.

BYERS: You seem like a nice young man, Mr. Lamb.

LAMB: Yes, sir, I do.

BYERS: You and your wife are soon going to be parents.

> LAMB *looks at* PICKER, *who nods his approval to answer.*

LAMB: We are, sir.

BYERS: How did you feel about being told you were to violate the vows you'd taken, to go back on the trust expected of a public servant?

LAMB: To be honest, it made me very uncomfortable, sir.

BYERS: Did you tell that to Mr. Slaughter?

LAMB: I did. He said the President had felt the same way. At first, anyway.

BYERS: The President? The President took orders from Mr. Slaughter, was that what he explicitly implied?

LAMB: That seemed to be the gist of his drift, yes, sir.

BYERS: The Director of the CIA controlled the President of the United States? That's the impression you came away with?

LAMB: No, sir. Mr. Slaughter expanded my ignorance to exclude any independent impressions.

BYERS: And just what was the CIA's interest in MPI, did the Director allow you to know that?

LAMB: Master Pictures, at the time of the takeover, was involved in the production of several feature films, but there was one in particular that caught Mr. Slaughter's eye.

BYERS: Mr. Slaughter was intimate with the studio's production schedule?

LAMB: Nothing escaped Mr. Slaughter's attention. Even as he spoke that day, he was being fed secret intelligence intravenously. His orders were that I was to hold on to MPI and that I was to stand by for further directives.

BYERS: And then?

LAMB: There was no then.

BYERS: That was it?

LAMB: A nurse came in to remove a tube from — a certain part of his anatomy that I would not like to go into in mixed company, sir.

BYERS: He said no more.

LAMB: No, sir. It was over and out. I just left, with the

understanding that we would not meet again as soon as possible.

BYERS: This would be at Mr. Slaughter's bedside once again.

LAMB: No, sir. The next time he talked to me, Mr. Slaughter had already died.

BYERS: Mr. Slaughter was dead?

LAMB: He was, yes, sir.

Reactions from all. BOWMAN *raps his gavel.*

BOWMAN [*To* LAMB]: He was medically dead?

LAMB: Head to toe-tag, yes, sir.

BOWMAN: My distinquished colleague will forgive me for interrupting.

BYERS: I would expect no less, Mr. Chairman.

BOWMAN: It's just that I am *most* anxious to hear what took place in connection with the witness's non-discussion with the then non-Mr. Slaughter.

PICKER: I remind the Chair that truth is sometimes stranger than fiction.

BOWMAN: The Chair needs no reminders of what a stranger truth is around here, sir! Mr. Lamb? Please continue on.

LAMB: Well, to start with, upon arriving at the hospital as having been previously instructed to, I was immediately informed that Mr. Slaughter had passed away as a result of dying.

BOWMAN: Were you told of what?

LAMB: No, I wasn't.

BOWMAN: And you didn't ask?

LAMB: I'm not cleared to have that kind of curiosity, sir. The Director had been kicked upstairs, was the way it was put to me.

BOWMAN: By whom? Whom else was there?

LAMB: Only Mrs. Slaughter, and members of the immediate Agency. Nevertheless, I was informed that Mr. Slaughter still wanted to see me. Quite honestly, I couldn't help feeling honored that I was one of the first people Mr. Slaughter had asked to see after he'd passed away.

BOWMAN: And just who was it who informed you that the late Mr. Slaughter would be keeping his appointment with you?

LAMB: It was Major Battle, sir.

BOWMAN: Major Manley Battle?

LAMB: Yes, sir, Major Manley Battle.

CROWD [*Overlapping*]: Major Battle!
Here we go!
It's time for prime time!
Film at eleven!

BOWMAN [*Gavels, then*]: Would you know if Major Battle is assigned to the CIA, Mr. Lamb?

LAMB: I believe that's one of the things I don't know any more, sir.

BOWMAN: Major Battle is, in fact, a member of the staff of NCS of the NSC, is he not? The National Council of Security for the National Security Council?

LAMB: I believe so, sir, as best I'm still able to understand anything at all, any more.

BOWMAN: And yet, you say Major Battle was your contact in connection with this occasion?

LAMB: He was, yes, sir.

BOWMAN: What happened then, after Major Battle told you of Mr. Slaughter's "promotion?"

LAMB: The Major escorted me to Mr. Slaughter's room, sir, where the bed had been emptied of him.

BOWMAN: And were you informed as to where the former Director had been redirected?

LAMB: I believe that what I understood, sir, was that Mr. Slaughter's remains were to be perpetually shifted from one grave to another. Because he had made so many countless enemies throughout his lifelong dedication to impose democracy on helpless people everywhere, there were understandable fears that in the event of a conventional burial, Mr. Slaughter's body might be taken hostage by terrorists and his family would never see him dead again.

BOWMAN: Can you tell us how Mr. Slaughter was able to communicate with you, given the loss of his voice, to say nothing of his life?

LAMB: It was accomplished electronically, sir. The Director had previously taped a video cassette for the express purpose of updating me beyond his own expiration date, as well as answers to any questions that occurred to him that he thought might occur to me. The essence of his message was that I was to take my orders from Major Battle during the time that Mr. Slaughter had been scheduled to be dead, or his "down time," as he put it.

> MERRY CHASE *looks at a slip of paper handed to her by a* TV CREW MEMBER, *then*:

MERRY CHASE [*To camera*]: A White House spokesman has just issued a statement stating that whatever truth to the contrary, Wiley Slaughter enjoyed a peaceful death, and that in a private ceremony, the Slaughter family followed the former CIA chief's instructions that his body be shredded.

BOWMAN: Mr. Lamb, the Committee is most grateful for your appearance.

LAMB: And I am for its, as well, sir.

> MERRY CHASE *is handed a second slip of paper, which she reads, to camera.*

MERRY CHASE: This just in! Total Network News has just learned from Cable Network News that the Committee's next witness is to be the Secretary of State, Mr. Bishop. This news is expected to reach the Committee some time later today.

BOWMAN [*To* LAMB]: You have provided this Committee, as well as your country, with a perfect example of innocence led astray, of blind acceptance transformed into immoral mindlessness.

LAMB: Then it was not all for nothing. Thank you, sir.

BOWMAN: Thank you, Mr. Lamb.

> *As* LAMB *and* MRS. LAMB *exit,* MERRY CHASE *gets the attention of* SECRETARY BISHOP, *on his way to the witness table.*

MERRY CHASE: Excuse me, Mr. Secretary? [*To camera*] With me now, Secretary of State Bishop. [*To* BISHOP] You've agreed to appear before the Committee, sir?

BISHOP: I never stop appearing before committees. I haven't been out of this building in two years.

MERRY CHASE: Mr. Secretary, you're on record as having been against the entire Mastergate operation.

BISHOP: I have, indeed. From the very beginning, I thought it was lunatic to use a movie company as a cover for diverting arms.

MERRY CHASE: And yet, you played a major role in the plan, sir.

BISHOP: That is a gross exaggeration. My involvement was strictly limited to the extent of my participation.

MERRY CHASE: But, sir, isn't it true that — ?

BISHOP [*Cuts in*]: I'm sorry, Merry. The truth will have to wait until after I finish testifying.

MERRY CHASE: Thank you, Mr. sir. [*To camera, as* BISHOP *goes to the witness table and is sworn in*] And so, as he joins the parade of witnesses, the question is, will Secretary of State Bishop, his well-known leaks to one side, will he be as outspoken for the record as often as he has been off in the past?

BOWMAN: Good afternoon, Mr. Secretary.

BISHOP: Senator.

BOWMAN: The Chair is most impressed by the courage you have shown by appearing before the Committee without benefit of counsel or a wife.

BISHOP: When you don't have anything to hide, I find you generally don't need anyone to do it behind.

BOWMAN: Quite right, sir. Quite right. Senator Knight, will you begin your questions?

KNIGHT: I thank the Chairman. I, too, would add an extension of thanks to the Secretary for his being here today. Mr. Secretary.

BISHOP: Senator.

MERRY CHASE [*To camera*]: There's very little love lost between these two, Secretary Bishop having been given a rough time earlier this week when he appeared before Senator Knight's Committee on Hindsight and Déjà Vu.

KNIGHT: Mr. Secretary, some six months to half a year ago, you were questioned by the Subcommittee of this Committee. Do you recall your appearance at that particular time?

BISHOP: I believe I looked pretty much as I do now.

KNIGHT: And do you remember our discussing the Mastergate situation at that particular frame in time?

BISHOP: Senator, we discussed a great many subjects, as I may or may not be able to recall. If you could possibly re-load your question, sir?

KNIGHT: You testified then that you were categorically opposed to the entire Mastergate idea.

BISHOP: Yes, I believe I testified to that.

KNIGHT: Oh, you did, sir.

BISHOP: Then I'll take my word for it.

KNIGHT: And yet, subsequently and prior, and all the times in between, you did all that you could to make the plan succeed, is that not also true?

BISHOP: Yes, sir, that's also so.

KNIGHT: Wouldn't you say that that was sending out a somewhat scrambled signal, sir?

BISHOP: Not at all. Since everyone knew I was against the plan, I assumed everyone would know that I was against whatever it was I was doing.

KNIGHT: Forgive me, sir, but how could you hope to convince anyone that you were opposed to something you were so busy supporting?

BISHOP: By resigning as often as I could — without actually damaging my effectiveness on the job.

KNIGHT: The job of implementing policies you had no particular faith in?

BISHOP: The Secretary of State doesn't spend his time just attending state funerals and going to poison gas conferences. It's not all fun and games, you know.

KNIGHT: It didn't trouble you, all the carrying on that was going on, is that what you're saying, sir?

BISHOP: It's my guess that I am, yes.

KNIGHT: It is exactly what you are saying, if I'm any judge of what I'm hearing.

BISHOP: Senator, at the very onslaught to this matter, I issued a strict appeal that I was to remain as completely uninformed as possible about this entire operation, so that I could maintain a perfectly honest front about what was going on behind my back.

KNIGHT: And just how did you put your ignorance into action?

BISHOP: I was content to let Mr. Slaughter make whatever arrangements were being made with the person with whom he was making them with.

KNIGHT: And with whom would that person have been in the person of?

BISHOP: Vice President Burden.

This news causes a stir.

KNIGHT: With Vice President Burden himself?

BISHOP: As I recall remembering, yes, sir.

KNIGHT: The Director of the CIA was dealing with the

Vice President?

BISHOP: Before you jump to any conclusions, I hasten to add that the Vice President personally assured me that even though he approved of these arrangements, he can prove he knew nothing about them, since he was in the room at the time they were made.

KNIGHT: If the Vice President was present, how does that square with the fact that the Vice President has said repeatedly that he never knew of the plan?

BISHOP: I take that to mean that he knew of it until such time as it became impossible for him to know that he did.

KNIGHT: Would you say that the Vice President was there in the capacity of acting for the President?

BISHOP: The President needs no help with his acting, sir.

KNIGHT: Would it be your opinion that the President knew that the Vice President knew?

BISHOP: Knew what?

KNIGHT: Everything that he didn't know.

BISHOP: No one else was in a position not to know as much as the President didn't.

KNIGHT: The President had no idea that his people

eventually pumped a billion dollars — one billion dollars — into the so-called filming of a movie, but actually for the purpose of purchasing illicit arms? [*To* BISHOP's *discomfort*] You have a grave responsibility, sir, to explain to the American people, right here and now, why those of you who had the President's ear chose to pull the wool over his eyes.

BISHOP: May I remind the Chair of our agreement that my appearance here today would, perforce, be limited, due to a prior commitment of long standing, which national security interests prohibit any further clarification of?

BOWMAN: Thank you, Mr. Secretary. The Chair so remembers. I'm afraid I'll have to cut you off, Senator Knight. You are accordingly excused, Mr. Secretary.

BISHOP: Thank you, Mr. Chairman. [*In farewell*] Senator Knight.

KNIGHT: Mr. Secretary.

BISHOP: I can't however leave, Mr. Chairman, without staying to say that I admit, yes, mistakes were made, I'll give you that. But never forget that it's hearings such as these which make it so hard for us to reach out to the business world to recruit those with managerial experience to make this Government work. You can't take these people out of the corporate sector and suddenly make them become answerable for their actions. It is hearings such as these which make it inevitable for private citizens to become public embarrassments. [*A pause*]

Yes, mistakes were made. Some dreadful ones. But they were honest mistakes. Honestly made. Honestly dreadful. I think this Committee ought to realize that if we're going to punish those who made them, we're only making it harder and harder to attract the people who will make the mistakes of the future. Thank you, Mr. Chairman.

BOWMAN: Thank you, Mr. Secretary.

As BISHOP *exits:*

CROWD[*Overlapping*]: I don't know how he gets away with it.
Bugger's smooth as silk.
I've got to read the transcript.
So what the hell was he for?
Whatever he was against.

> MERRY CHASE *has rushed to interview* MAJOR BATTLE, *ramrod stiff and resplendent in full Marine uniform, service ribbons overflowing, a bible in one hand.* MRS. BATTLE *stands beside him, holding a cloth carry bag.*

MERRY CHASE [*To camera*]: With me now, to give us a minute, is the man of the hour, Major Manley Battle. [*Offering him her mike*] Major.

BATTLE: Merry.

MERRY CHASE: Major. You are the Committee's next witness, sir.

BATTLE: They gave me an order I couldn't refuse, Merry.

MERRY CHASE: I see Mrs. Battle's going to be at your side today?

BATTLE: My wife and I're used to going through hell together, Merry.

MERRY CHASE: Do you believe it's right for anyone, as some have suggested you have, to break the law of the land, Major?

BATTLE: Merry, I didn't fight in Korea and Vietnam and a number of other countries, which I'm still contractually forbidden to mention; I didn't have the privilege of watching more than one mother's son die again and again in my arms, to suddenly decide not to uphold this country's laws. That was explicit the day I had this uniform tailored.

As the BATTLES *head for the witness table:*

MERRY CHASE: Thank you, Major Battle, Mrs. Battle. [*To camera*] The Committee, in the half hour Major Battle has consented to grant them, is expected to focus on the Major's role in what came to be known as "Operation Masterplan," which the Major kicked off by accompanying former witness, Abel Lamb, on his trip to Los Angeles. Here is Senator Bowman.

> BATTLE *has taken his seat, having been sworn in, using his own bible.* MRS. BATTLE *sits behind him.*

His attorney, BOYLE, *is at his side.*

BOWMAN: Mr. Hunter, would you please to begin?

HUNTER: Thank you, Mr. Chairman. April 15th of last year, Major: does that date ring a nerve?

BATTLE: Loud and clear, yes, sir.

HUNTER: That was the date on which you flew to California along with Mr. Lamb, is that correct, Major?

BATTLE: Mr. Lamb traveled by commercial carrier. Standing orders forbid me to fly on anything but a Stealth bomber.

HUNTER: That certainly goes Business Class one better, I would say.

Laughter from the crowd.

BOYLE: Mr. Hunter is perfectly aware that, due to the Major Battle's furtive activities, in order to maintain the strictest security, the Major is required to fly, drive and even walk underneath any possible detection by radar.

BOWMAN: The Committee is not insensitive to the Major's sensitive position, Mr. Boyle, nor is it unaware that the Major sports an extremely high profile in one media or the other for someone who's supposed to stay so close to the ground.

BATTLE: Publicity is a small price to pay for secrecy, sir.

BOWMAN: That I'll grant you. Proceed ahead, Mr. Hunter.

HUNTER: What exactly was your purpose in semi-accompanying Mr. Lamb to California, Major, paying special attention to the truth, if you will?

BATTLE: I was there to ride shotgun for him. To supervise the duck alignment.

HUNTER: To put them all in a row.

BATTLE: Affirmative.

HUNTER: In plain English, if memory serves, will you please describe the meeting that Mr. Lamb convened upon his arrival in California?

BATTLE: It was scheduled for oh-eight hundred hours at the Master Motion Pictures Studios with the late Mr. Rob Merritt, CEO of MPI.

HUNTER: And would you have known what was said at that time?

BATTLE: Every word. Miles away, ostensibly enjoying a martini in the Polo Lounge of the Beverly Hills, my "olive" allowed me to eavesdrop on their conversation electronically.

HUNTER: Mr. Lamb had been wired, is that what you're saying?

BATTLE: One of his gold chains was bugged. He wore four. One for receiving, one for sending, while the third contained an anti-jamming device to scramble any possible bugging by either the KGB or CBS. The fourth was just for show.

HUNTER: You had every base covered.

BATTLE: Vigilance is piece work, sir. Mr. Lamb's suit had been made with specially treated threads that acted as microtransmitters, so that we always knew the precise position of his location, providing that he was never more than six feet away from his clothes, which happened quite regularly, once we got to Hollywood. After putting down at LAX, Mr. Lamb was limmoed by secured stretch to MPI, to pay a courtesy call on the aforesaid Mr. Merritt, and to personally hand him the resignation speech Mr. Merritt was to deliver, as well as a first draft of his suicide note.

HUNTER: All of which preceded the point at which Mr. Lamb took over at the studio.

BATTLE: He became chief dog-in-charge, yes, sir.

HUNTER: He ran the studio.

BATTLE: He did.

HUNTER: And you ran Mr. Lamb.

BATTLE: As per Mr. Slaughter's pre- and post-death orders.

BOWMAN: Mr. Hunter, having spent your span of time, I will ask you to yield the questioning to Senator Bunting, if you will.

HUNTER: Thank you, Mr. Chairman.

BOWMAN: Thank you, Mr. Hunter. Senator Bunting.

BUNTING: Thank you, Mr. Chairman. Thank you, Mr. Hunter.

BOWMAN: Thank you, Senator.

HUNTER [*Overlapping*]: Thank you, Senator.

BUNTING: Major.

BATTLE: Senator.

BUNTING: Let us get to the heart of the meat, shall we, Major?

BATTLE: Ready on the firing line, sir.

BUNTING: I ask you to turn your attention — a position, I might add, at which you stand magnificently — to the production schedule at Master Studios at the time of the Government's engobblement. In particular, a proposed picture show, entitled "Tet!, the Movie," dealing with the Veet Cong offensive in which our B-1 bombers proved helpless against their godless 10-speed bikes because Congress had not shown enough gumption to allow surgically selective air strikes against the enemy's most residential districts.

BOWMAN: May I ask the Senator to kindly stop raking over dead horses?

BOYLE: And may I remind the Senator of the Major's familiarity with the Tet offensive, having led his command in several heroic assaults on that occasion, including one against his own men.

BUNTING: I yield to no man in bowing to the height of the debt in spilled blood that this nation owes Major Battle, whose many decorations spill over onto your very own chest, sir.

> BOYLE *thrusts his chest forward proudly and we become aware that he is wearing several military medals, the overflow from* BATTLE'*s uniform.*

In fact, I would be highly remissive in not reading into the record the Major's remarkable recipiency of multiple military awards, including — [*Consulting his notes*] — the Bronze Star. [BOYLE, *using his pencil, points to a ribbon on* BATTLE'*s chest*] The Purple Heart. [BOYLE'*s pencil goes to the proper ribbon*] The Meritorious Service Medal. [BOYLE *points it out*] And the Legion of Merit. [BOYLE *points to that medal. It's on his own chest*] All of which he earned during his two hours in Vietnam.

BATTLE [*Correcting him*]: Tours, sir.

BUNTING: Pardon?

BATTLE: Two tours, not two hours.

BUNTING: Yes, of course, but it's still kind of impressive, anyway.

BATTLE: No quarrel, sir.

BUNTING: Tell us, then, if you would, what you can, Major, about "Tet!"

BATTLE: "Tet! the Movie," or Tet, the for real, sir?

BUNTING: "Tet! the Movie," if you please.

BATTLE: Yes, sir. It was originally conceived as a high-budgeted action film, with a good deal of war footage and bloodshed, to be ready in time for a Christmas release.

BUNTING: And what exactly was the budget at the time of the movie's conceivement?

BATTLE: Forty million dollars. Which is considered a lot of money in Hollywood, sir.

BUNTING: I'm sure it is.

BATTLE: I, as it turned out, was aware of "Tet!, the Movie," not only from my own first hand-to-hand experience in Vietnam, but also from having read "Tet!," the book, in manuscript form at the CIA, before the agency had decided who the author was going to be. The story dealt with a young American soldier who achieves his manhood by setting fire to a village schoolhouse, filled with Viet Cong posing as five-year-olds. Originally, the picture's shooting location was to be the Philippines, where for a monetary consideration, as much napalm and Agent Orange as necessary would be dropped on the Philippine countryside and its inhabitants, such was the level of cooperation between Washington and the then-residents of the presidential palace in Manila, or Neiman-Marcos, as it was called in-house. However, at Mr. Slaughter's direction, it was decided to shoot the movie in San Elvador.

BUNTING: That would be the Republic of San Elvador.

BATTLE: It would.

BUNTING: I wonder if I might ask you to use the map we have here for the purpose of your using it, Major. If I could just ask my niece and nephew to roll it out, please?

BATTLE: Yes, sir.

> *Two* PAGES *roll out the map.* BATTLE *crosses to it and picks up a wooden pointer, as the flashbulbs begin popping. After a bit of discreet but unmistakable posing:*

San Elvador lies just right of center here in Central America. It has a democratic form of government that has been run by its Army for the past forty years.

Passionately anti-communist, with a vigorous opposition press, a strong, vocal church and free elections that are promised regularly. But most geo-politically significant, there is San Elvador's unmistakable proximity-ship to its immediate neighbor to its far left, Ambigua.

BUNTING: Ambigua is totalitarily Lenin-Marxist, in your opinion, Major?

BATTLE: It's as red as the ace of hearts, sir. The whole nine yardski.

BUNTING: And completely controlled by Moscow?

BATTLE: Does the Pope ride an encyclical? [CROWD *laughs*] Not that I mean to make light of the Communist menace. Or the Catholics, either.

BUNTING: Major, I'm sure that this Committee, as well as the country for which we stand, would be most appreciative for you to share some of your invaluable daylight with us on that sad, proud and benighted land.

BATTLE: Yes, sir. The Republic of Ambigua, or La Republica de Ambigua, is yet another in a string of betrayed revolutions wherein a legitimate set of high ideals were once more cruelly twisted and cynically Sovietized. The United States has had a long period of the most intimate relations with the Ambiguan government, the last eighteen of Ambigua's presidents being West Point graduates. But a coup occurred and the reins of power changed hands three years ago when the former President of Ambigua, General Delinqua, and the country's Prime Minister, Mrs. Delinqua, were in New York on an emergency shopping trip, at which point the Government was taken over by a Dr. Overtega, a former podiatrist and his band of foot soldiers.

BUNTING: The United State was quick to immediately recognize the new Overtega government, did we not?

BATTLE: Self-interest begins at home, sir. The US Air Force has thousands of personnel in Ambigua, learning the ABC's of our IBM's, manning our most highly secret missile silos positioned here — [*Pointing at map*] and here — which place us logistically just a nucular hop, skip and jump away from any one of a thousand Communist countries. It was and remains imperative that the US maintain its ability to liais militarily with whatever Ambiguan infrastructure is in power. Within hours of seizing the Presidential throne, Overtega ordered a Government-staged protest, where 8-by-10 pictures of John Wayne, part of the foreign aid we had shipped them, were burned by crowds carrying "Satan, Go Home!" signs. I was immediately inserted in-country, where I established a Delta Squad beachhead just a stone's throw from the US Embassy. Five thousand American souls were evacced out, sir, their departure causing the population of Ambigua to instantly double. With our people gone, Ambigua became a venerable Red Sea. Overnight, a landing strip was built to accomodate the most advanced Soviet bombers, planes so fast, a Russian pilot could eat a burrito in Ambigua and wash it down with a bowl of borscht in Lenin's Tomb. Soviet military adviseniks armed the Elvadorians with vast quantities of automatic Baryshnikovs, ground-to-air rockets and heat-seeking machetes. But most provocatively, and least acceptably, they dug underground nucular missile silos below *our* nucular missile silos so that we were in danger of being the first military force in history to ever be attacked simultaneously from behind *and* from below.

BUNTING: And, all the while, this country, the most powerful nation in the land, stood by, just sucking on its blanket?

BATTLE: Only semi-so, sir. There was a constant stab at efforts to appeal to Overtega to fold his country back into democracy.

BUNTING: Including a stab at Overtega himself, am I right?

BATTLE: We tried everything from private persuasion to public assassination.

BUNTING: Despite the fact that there are those who think the CIA has no business assassinating anyone; who prefer to mollycoddle those who would murder America in its bed, if they could get away with it?

BATTLE: There are those who think Garbageoff's got a cute forehead, sir.

Laughter from the CROWD.

BUNTING: Exactly.

BOWMAN: I wonder if we might not backtrack to the subject of Ambigua, Major.

BATTLE: Yes, sir. What we finally scoped in on as our best hope was a group of idealistic Ambigualitos, still loyal to the Delinquan government, hiding in the hills in St. Tropez, and willing to make any sacrifice to overthrow the overthrow, to once more make the People's Republic the Republic of the People.

BUNTING: This was the group known as the "Los Otros?"

BATTLE: Yes, sir. The "Los Otros." "The Others." A rag-tag band of guerrilla fighters, badly in need of humanitarian aid and arms such as rifles, grenades, mortars, jeeps and gun ships.

BUNTING: And what sort of humanitarian aid?

BATTLE: Uh — [*Stuck for a moment, then*] Medicine. Blankets. Plus the necessary rocket launchers, tanks and napalm to protect those blankets.

BUNTING: Congress, of course, had approved this aid, had it not?

BATTLE: It had.

BUNTING: To the tune of some one hundred million dollars.

BATTLE: No tune is too high to pay for liberty, sir.

BUNTING: And yet, six months later, the very same Congress refused to vote more assistance to the Los Otros, correct, Major?

BATTLE: Correct and disgraceful, sir.

BUNTING: Disgraceful is a very strong word, Major.

BATTLE: I believe this particular shoe happens to fit like a glove, sir.

CROWD[*Overlapping*]: How gung ho can you get?
The old man's not going to let him get away with this!
Ted Koppel's got to be salivating!

BOWMAN[*To* BUNTING]: Senator, I resent your partisan egging on of the defendant!

BOYLE [*Getting to his feet*]: You mean witness!

BOWMAN: You sit down!

BUNTING [*Angrily, to* BOWMAN]: Your chicken behavior has come home to roost, sir!

BATTLE [*To* BOWMAN, *even angrier, standing*]: You play with firepower, you get burned, Senator!

BOWMAN: We're not here to hurl bumper stickers at one another, Major! [*By now, the room is in an uproar. To* BATTLE] You will kindly sit!

BOYLE: The Major has no problem standing up for

America, Mr. Chairman!

As BATTLE *takes his seat:*

BUNTING: Indeed, he has not!

MRS. BATTLE *takes her needles and yarn from her tote bag and picks up knitting an American flag. Referring to a large painting that hangs behind the Committee:*

Major Battle, sitting here in the shadow of this magnificent portrait of our Founding Fathers — a fine example of the kind of art that a man can take his whole family to watch — it is all that I can say — although I know it doesn't go for everyone here — but this is a big country, Major, and it never forgets. And what it won't remember, I can assure you, are those among us who have singled you out for scathing for merely doing your duty. We may all applaud Washington crossing the Delaware, but when Washington starts crossing fine officers such as yourself, sir, I consider it both a shame and my honor to apologize on behalf of all those countless men, women and especially children, who've been left without a prayer in our school system, who need heroes to grow up to, role models that don't come better than your own gallant wife's husband. Hang in there, sir. There are millions of us in your platoon! [*Standing to salute him*] Proud and honored to serve America's only four-star Major!

BOWMAN: Thank you, Senator Bunting, for your most objective presentation of your own point of view.

BUNTING: Thank *you*, Mr. Chairman.

BOWMAN [*Wearily*]: I must say, I find it a sad commentary on these hearings that we should so quickly participate in the sinking of our bipartisanship. No American is more American than any other American. I am even more disturbed than usual by outbursts of displays by any of my colleagues trying to prove he is gung-holier than thou. I would hope that our next questioner will bear it in mind that there is a certain degree of fairness that the nation expects this Committee to exemplarize. Representative Sellers? If you please, sir.

SELLERS: Thank you, Mr. Chairman. Major Battle.

BATTLE: Sir.

MERRY CHASE [*To camera*]: Congressman Sellers, himself a Vietnam vet, having flown several missions into Hanoi with Jane Fonda.

SELLERS: Major Battle, while we're still in a tributary vein, sir, I'd like to add my chorus of approval for your many years of outspoken devotion to the defense of this country, which I, as a fellow serviceman, have also devoted countless weekends to.

BATTLE: Every little bit helps, sir.

SELLERS: America is indeed a land worth fighting for, is it not, Major?

BATTLE: I've got a head full of shrapnel to prove it, sir.

SELLERS: Can you think of another one anywhere where members of the armed forces are free to publicly vocalize their criticism of the actions of the legislature?

BATTLE: Zip, sir. None.

SELLERS: With that in mind, can you, if you can, implify your amplication that the Congress's decision to deny donating additional aid to the Los Otros was — [*Consulting his notes*] "disgraceful." That was it, Major? Disgraceful? That was the epitaph you just hurled, was it not?

BATTLE: I consider the word a direct hit, sir. Without further monetary-stroke-military aid, scores of Ambiguan freedom lovers, who had gone way out on their life and limbs for us, were literally cut off at the knees without a paddle.

SELLERS: Ah, but not quite, as it turned out, inasmuch as Mr. Slaughter managed to "save" the day, did he not, wouldn't you say, in fact, have you already repeatedly not?

BATTLE: Underline "saved," sir. Mr. Slaughter, having assessed San Elvador's extreme adjacentness alongside Ambigua, saw its immediate possibility as a base for supplying the Los Otros, using the primitive jungle highway which connects the two nations and known as the Mao Che Minh Trail.

SELLERS: Thereby permitting the United States to continue to supply the resistance with arms and humanitarian aid?

BATTLE: As the pipeline had considerably narrowed, we were only able to supply aid that was inhumanitarian.

SELLERS: The operation was immediately green-lighted?

BATTLE: It was an instant go, yes, sir.

SELLERS: With you, of course, in charge.

BATTLE: Yes, sir.

SELLERS: With you, in turn, reporting to Mr. Slaughter.

BATTLE: When he was between comas, yes, sir. Otherwise, he was completely conscious of the fact that I was acting for him whenever he was not.

SELLERS: Were *you* conscious that Mr. Slaughter's plan had a major hitch, Major? That the Congress had voted against any and all additional aid to the Los Otros? Had, in fact, passed a law making it illegal to provide such assistance?

BATTLE: It's Congress's bat and ball, sir.

SELLERS: Nevertheless, you and the Director simply decided to do an end run around the Legislative Branch of the United States?

BATTLE: That's not exactly the way I would put it, sir.

SELLERS: And in what way exactly would you put it, Major?

BATTLE: I would say that that's when Operation Masterplan kicked in.

SELLERS: You prefer euphemisms, do you?

BATTLE: I prefer calling a spade by its code word, sir.

SELLERS: In whatever words you like, Major, suppose you scope us in on just exactly how Operation Masterplan worked.

BATTLE: That takes us back to "Tet!," sir.

SELLERS: The movie, the book, the war or the album?

BATTLE: "Tet!," the movie, sir. The shooting script called for several battle scenes between US and Viet Cong forces. Master Studios had purchased a certain amount of military hardware from several other movie companies, plus a great many additional weapons from certain Middle Eastern powers anxious to dump them because they came with so many instructions. Any rate, these battle sequences were scheduled to be filmed in southern San Elvador, at the point at which it borders on northern Ambigua. The plan was to ship somewhat more additional military supplies to the movie company than had been indicated in the script, and then to re-route them to the Los Otros encampments.

SELLERS: And just how much more than somewhat are

we talking about?

BATTLE: Eight hundred million dollars worth.

SELLERS: Eight hundred million dollars of unauthorized expenditure?

BATTLE: What price tag would *you* hang on the Statue of Liberty, sir?

SELLERS: This initial jump, this twenty-fold leap from the film's budget of forty to eight hundred million dollars, this didn't raise an eyebrow or two at the studio? If not among the Government employees, then certainly amongst the professional picture people?

BATTLE: The amount was finessed by cross collateralizing the difference over the cost of several other movies being made by MPI at the same time.

SELLERS: No one in Hollywood was any the wiser?

BATTLE: As a rule of thumb, no, sir.

SELLERS: Not even when later added costs to the making of the motion picture would finally escalate to one billion dollars?

BATTLE: One billion three, with the catering.

SELLERS: You were in San Elvador when the arms arrived, Major? To help divert them clandestinely to Ambigua?

BATTLE: I was operating under cover, in a change of identity mode.

SELLERS: You were not who you normally are?

BATTLE: I was not any one of those I've sometimes been. Mr. Slaughter had made it possible for me to act as his right arm, by putting me in the cast. Working in the film, I could be on the scene and *in* the scene at the same time.

SELLERS: And no one at all knew of this plan, except for those of you who wanted those of us not to. Not the Congress, not the press, not the American people.

BATTLE: None of the above, no, sir.

SELLERS: Major, you took an oath as an officer to obey your Commander-in-Chief, did you not?

BATTLE: I was standing right there when I did it, sir.

SELLERS: Would you feel it your duty if your Commander-in-Chief, the President of the United States, ordered you to break the law?

BATTLE: I do not believe my President would order me to do such a thing, not knowingly.

SELLERS: You have great faith in the President.

BATTLE: Yes, sir, I do. Whoever that President might be. And whenever he is, as well.

SELLERS: I want you to think hard, Major.

BATTLE: Starting when, sir?

SELLERS: Your answer could change the course of this nation's history.

BATTLE: I am always ready to, sir.

SELLERS: Did the President know of the Masterplan plan?

BATTLE: I was told he didn't know.

SELLERS: By whom?

BATTLE: By the same people who told *him* he didn't know.

SELLERS: And they would be who, would you know?

BATTLE: Key members of his staff; those players who keep track of what he knows, what he knew and what he never will. The people who have the President's memory at their fingertips.

SELLERS: The President, then, to the best of your knowledge, had absolutely none of his own.

BATTLE: He may have had knowledge of it, without knowing he did.

SELLERS: The President can't be expected to know

everything he knows, is that what you're saying?

BATTLE: It's hard enough for him to remember all that he doesn't.

SELLERS: In your opinion, did the President even know that the Overtega coup had ever taken place?

BATTLE: My own feeling, irregardless of my opinion, is that there was no reason for him to be informed on this matter. You can't swing a dead cat over your head without hitting some South, Central or Sub-American country that isn't revolting in some way or another. I don't know what purpose it would serve to wake the President every five minutes throughout his working day just to report however many coups might be occurring all over the map.

SELLERS: Tell me, Major: if you were the President, do you think *you* might possibly have liked to have known?

BOYLE: With all due respect, sir, Major Battle doesn't happen to be one of the men who *is* the President at this time.

SELLERS: I beg to differ, Mr. Boyle. I happen to think that Major Battle was the President more often than we'll ever know. As well as Secretary of State, of Defense, of God-knows-of-Secretary-of-what-else-and-whatever. Many a world leader has played with toy soldiers. What we have in Major Battle, I believe, is a soldier who played with toy leaders. Don't you think this country deserves better, Major?

BATTLE: I happen to think that this country deserves the very best, sir, although, in all honesty, it can't always be counted on to know what that is for itself. I take pride in being part of that tiny fistful of men who steal into the night that other Americans sleep so soundly through, to leave my wife and children every chance I get, riding point on missions contrived to keep this country in the win column against the Communists, half an eye always over our shoulder, hoping it's not too late to save this country before — [*Making quote signs with his fingers*] "Congress" passes a law against that, too! [*He stands, ready to leave.*]

> *Flashbulbs and general hubbub. As* MERRY CHASE *makes her way to, and interviews* BATTLE, BURDEN *makes his way to the witness table, greeting people as he does. His lawyer,* CARVER, *joins him*]

MERRY CHASE [*At* BATTLE's *side*]: Major Battle, I wonder if you would confirm or deny a rumor for us?

BATTLE: I'd be happy to do either, Merry.

MERRY CHASE: Did the President pre-pardon you for your role in Mastergate?

BATTLE: No, sir, Merry. A pardon suggests wrong doing. Even if the President did offer me one, my wife and I couldn't sleep in our cots at night if anyone of you out there with a candle in your heart for me thought I didn't know at what point my patriotism might turn criminal.

MERRY CHASE: You have no sense, no feeling at all, that perhaps you were set up to take the blame, to act as fall guy for the President?

BATTLE: Negative, Merry. And I'm totally prepared to spend the rest of my life out on the lecture circuit to prove it. [*He exits with* MRS. BATTLE]

MERRY CHASE [*To camera*]: After weeks of listening to hearing witnesses, the Committee seems to be climbing the ladder in its search for pay dirt. After trying so hard to learn who knew what and just how high those particular who were, this morning's witness — voluntary witness — can go a long way in filling in the answers [BOWMAN *gavels.*] Now, it's back to the Committee and its appearance before it of Vice President Burden.

> BURDEN, *having been sworn in, sits, as a Secret Service Man enters, ear plug in place, looks about, then signals offstage. A beat, then* MRS. BURDEN *enters, exchanges a kiss with* BURDEN, *waves to the crowd, then sits.*

HUNTER: Good morning, Mr. Vice President.

BURDEN: I've never woken to one I didn't like, Shep.

HUNTER: Would you care to make an opening statement, sir?

BURDEN: I might just make one when we're finished.

HUNTER: If I may, I'd like to begin by asking you about

the purchase of additional weapons and ammunition, sir.

BURDEN: Go for it.

HUNTER: It is true, is it not, Mr. Vice President, that the Administration, Congress having slammed the door in its face, additional fund-wise in terms of the guerrillas, turned around and created a secondary enterprise to replenish said dried-up funds, would that be a correct depiction of an assumption, sir?

BURDEN: You can't sit aroun' thinkin' instead of actin'. You can't just put history on hold, y'know. There's no snooze button on the American dream.

HUNTER: And this said replenishment was accomplished by inviting certain pivotal players to the Capitol to provide pivotal capital, is that also correct?

BURDEN: Well, rememberin' it in the best possible way I can, from time to time, Major Battle would fly up from the movie location fer the purpose of briefin' would-be contributors to the conflict on the progress of the fightin'.

HUNTER: It never struck you that a low-grade officer had finangled himself into matters of such high policy?

BURDEN: Major Battle is a hands-on, over-the-top, in-your-face, my kinda guy.

HUNTER: Did you know that the Major has consistently refused to take a lie detector test?

BURDEN: Omina tell you somepin', Mr. Counselor. Nobody ever asked the Major to take a polygraph when he was crawlin' on his belly through the mud to lead his men on an attack on Pearl Harbor.

> *A moment while* CARVER *whispers to* BURDEN *regarding his gaffe.* BURDEN *takes it in stride, smiles, and looks at* MRS. BURDEN, *who shakes her head in amusement.*

HUNTER: Sir, if we can, I would like to get back to the meetings.

BURDEN: Which ones? God, I'd like *you* to go to as many meetings as I do an' have any idea of what's goin' on.

HUNTER: The ones where the funds for Ambigua were raised. Can you tell us where they were held?

BURDEN: In the basement of the White House. Near the swimming pool. I believe the area had been Bebe Rebozo's dressing room at one time.

BOWMAN: And when Major Battle made his "pitch," did he speak to potential patrons of the war all by himself?

BURDEN: He did.

HUNTER: Mr. Vice President, isn't it true, sir, that you were sometimes there to help?

BURDEN: I was.

HUNTER: You confirm that.

BURDEN: I've never denied it, once I finally admitted it.

HUNTER: You were there often?

BURDEN: Not that many.

HUNTER: Once or twice?

BURDEN: The first two times. About eighty all together.

HUNTER: What about the President?

BURDEN [*With a sigh of resignation*]: I know.

HUNTER: No, no, did the President himself ever attend?

BURDEN: Not himself, no. He had so much trouble findin' the room, he finally lost interest.

HUNTER: Mr. Vice President, the amount collected from private donors was in excess of a hundred million dollars, for which the contributors received what, if anything, can you tell us, in exchange?

BURDEN: First off, they were invited to the Pentagon, where, along with the Joint Chiefs of Staff, they attended a prayer breakfast in the War Room, and then later, they each had their picture taken nappin' with the President.

HUNTER: They received one more item, if I'm not mistaken, Mr. Vice President?

BURDEN: Y'mean the cassette.

HUNTER: The video cassette that allegedly showed the Los Otros in action.

BURDEN: That's the baby.

HUNTER: Although, as we've since come to know, this motion picture footage was staged and shot by the motion picture company to create the impression that the *real* war was going swimmingly. This was the same footage, was it not, that was later fed to national television; seen throughout the country on the evening news, with the public under the impression that they were watching the real thing?

BURDEN: Omina clue ya in on somethin', okay? There's no expert worth his dose a' salts won't tell ya the American people have had a bellyfull of war footage. They just don't watch those kinda shows that close anymore. I mean, come on, after forty years of the same exposure on the box, your day in an' day out life 'n death struggles in the world are really just so much dinner-time background bang-bang. Still in all, it was felt there'd be more support fer the defeat of Overtega if the American people thought that we had any kinda chance at all of winnin' the movie.

HUNTER: You mean the war.

BURDEN [*Shrugs*]: Whatever.

HUNTER: Which, in the real world, Overtega's forces and not those we were supporting were, in fact, winning?

BURDEN: That's right. Which was, in the subtext of this content, why those of us who're encrusted with the sacred responsibility to see that freedom doesn't just get eroded out, third world-wise, were bustin' our heinies to replace the weapons that'd been lost by the Los Otros.

HUNTER: The Defense Department did not supply these replacements?

BURDEN: We were forced to look elsewhere.

HUNTER: Therefore, this second shipment of arms was supplied by —?

BURDEN: General Mendacio.

HUNTER: Juan Carlo Mendacio of Oblivia?

BURDEN: That's right.

HUNTER: Are we talking about General Mendacio, the so-called King of Cocaine?

BURDEN: No one is higher.

HUNTER: Mr. Vice President, I need some help, sir.

BURDEN: Talk to me, son.

HUNTER: If you could think of me as a human being rather than as a lawyer. How does a simple citizen reconcile such reckless cynicism as being consistent with the pristine and puritanical principles that we, as a people, purport to support? Forgive me, sir. That was not an easy thing to say.

BURDEN: No one seems to mind when the shoe is in the other foot, do they? When the right hand doesn't know what the left wing's doin'. Although, speakin' in a personal mode, I will tell you that I see no great harm in divergent differences. Heck, this country's met the challenge of fiercely oppositional pointa views many times in our history, an' I didn't see us comin' out any the worse for the exercise.

HUNTER: You have some specific example in mind, Mr. Vice President?

BURDEN: Well, certainly, the Civil War, for one.

BOWMAN: In which tens of thousands of Americans killed each other? You don't think we didn't come out any the worse for it, sir?

BURDEN: But at least it cleared the air, y'know what I'm sayin'?

BOWMAN: So that we're very clear about this Mendacio

business, Mr. Vice President: are you telling us that this government, the government of the United States, the government of Washington, Jefferson, Lincoln, Nebraska, Iowa, Texas, the Maine, the Marne, of Tippecanoe and Truman, too, this same Government made a done deal with an acknowledged and despicable drugpin?

BURDEN: Senator, before we nail this fella inta the ground, I'd like to remind the Committee that for years General Mendacio has provided the United States with a miasma of services.

BOWMAN: And, as a result, he's amassed a vast mass of arms large enough to sell us one hundred million dollars worth?

BURDEN: Well, ya gotta remember a lot of it was weapons this nation sold to various countries to help stop the General's drug trafficking, which weapons naturally became his after he managed to buy the governments of those various countries from profits he made selling drugs to this nation.

BOWMAN: So it was really the money from people with needles in their arms which paid for the additional arms that were flown down to the Los Otros?

BURDEN: That's right. Flown down in an airborne manner in a number of unmarked planes, each of which was repainted several times in mid-air. Unfortunately, just prior to the planes settin' down, the entire shipment hit the fan. Due, of course, to the unexpected attack by the Los Otros on the Embassy.

BOWMAN: Our Embassy?

BURDEN: Well, what it was was that it was the movie set of the US Embassy that was attacked.

BOWMAN: I confess to a slight logic lag, sir. Why on earth an attack on an American Embassy, real or otherwise, by the very people we were trying to help? Why would they bite the hand that arms them?

BURDEN: Wake up an' smell the coffee, Senator. It was their way of protesting Congress's wishy-washy aid cut-off. Uncognizant that that funding fer their cause had gone private, they didn't have a clue that, weaponry-wise, they were about to get a fresh blast of sunshine pumped up their skirts. They were warned that their actions were bound to doom any future aid and, for a certainty, they would never work in another movie again. But it meant nothin' to them, availwise. They answered by blowin' up the Embassy. Both the set *an'* the real one. On a positive note, if I may: thanks to all the years of our training them, the Los Otros fought magnificently that day, even though it was us they were fightin'. The fact that they were able to inflict so many casualties among those who taught them how was proof that our money hadn't been totally wasted.

BOWMAN: The net result of all of which was that the motion picture, "Tet!, the Movie," was never finished?

BURDEN: Well, with the resistance turned against us, we

pulled out altogether, 'cept for leavin' behind a styro-foam movie set representin' the front of an American high school standin', with the hope that it would be used to further the education of all children in the region.

BOWMAN: So it was all for naught, sir? All your illicit solicitations? Your countless Congressional trans-gressions? All the squandered lives and laundered dol-lars, all for naught, sir? All for naught?

BURDEN: Mr. Chairman. Other members of the rest of the Committee. There's somepin' I think's been pretty well lost sight of in these hearings. There's somepin' a whole lot here way besides blame that's the cause a' what happened. And it's not called blame at all. It's called "seizin' the initiative," that's what it is. We didn't ask the British, "Please, sir, can we become a nation?" No, sir. If we hadn't of broken every law in the books back in Seventeen Seventy-whenever, if we hadn't done the Revolution thing and stayed English, each one of us woulda had to have driven to Capitol Hill here today on the left side of the road — and our President woulda been a Queen!

> *Flashbulbs, crowd reactions. He exits with* MRS. BURDEN *and the Secret Service Man.*

BOWMAN [*After gaveling for order*]: The Committee is most grateful to the Vice President for appearing as our final witness. Ending as we are the public portion of these hearings, I would also like to expel the virtues of the Committee itself in completing the very arduous challenge which it originally set out to. Now follows the process of deliberation, of gestation and legislation — [*Mike static causes only intermittent words of his to be heard*] We will scrutinize to the fullest — [*The lights start flickering*] We will tamper with mercy — what is happening here??

> *By now the TV monitors have gone haywire, as well.*

MERRY CHASE [*To camera*]: Ladies and gentlemen, we seem to be experiencing some technical difficulties. We're going to return you to our studios until — [TNN DIRECTOR *gives her a hand signal*] Oh? Right. [*To camera*] I've just been told we can't do that. Something extraordinary seems to be happening here. [*The room is plunged into darkness*] There seems to be some sort of interference. We've lost our picture temporarily. No one can quite — [*Art card on monitors reads: TECHNICAL DIFFICULTIES - PLEASE STAND BY*] I don't know if I can be heard. I know I can't be seen. Whatever it is seems to be quite beyond our control.

> *Suddenly, center stage,* WYLIE SLAUGHTER *"appears," in a flickering, eerie overhead light, wearing a short, patient's hospital gown, bare legged, his feet in black scuffs. He wears a short-sleeved white shirt, one or two sizes too big and, of course, the requisite red necktie. A hospital patient's ID on one wrist, several IV tubes hang from his arms. He leans on a shiny, stainless steel walker.* MRS. SLAUGHTER, *veiled, in black, sits behind him.*

SLAUGHTER: Don't touch your sets! Stay where you are!

His other-worldly, ghost-like image is seen on the monitors.

MERRY CHASE [*To the camera*]: Incredible as it may seem, the hearing room has been rocked by the sudden appearance of the late Director of the CIA!

A barrage of flashbulbs.

SLAUGHTER: I am Wylie Grimm Slaughter. September 24th, 1904 — April 3rd, 1989. Having anticipated this hearing, I took great pains to produce what you see here before you — a holographic image that creates the illusion that I am present in this room, whereas you all know that I've passed away for reasons you've read in newspaper accounts, accounts prepared under my specific mis-direction. I will, of course, answer no questions here today. This is no time for me to learn new tricks. Swearing me in, were it even remotely possible, would serve as little purpose now as it ever did in the past. I am not here to plead ignorance or to pass the buck. I am here to take responsibility for it all; to *bask* in your blame! At this moment in time — *your* time — Operation Masterplan will have self-destructed to the gleeful satisfaction of the media, those self-anointed guardians of the nation's interest. Let me state this one last time that I have never been opposed to the belief that the press had the right to print or broadcast everything it knows. I simply maintain that they don't have to know *everything*. If putting the freedom of this nation ahead of freedom for the press is a crime, then I am guilty! If putting the US ahead of the UP is treason, then wake up the firing squad! For me, any means whatsoever is permissible to stave off the mortal danger that was posed when the first Red Dawn darkened the sky shining down on Karl Marx, as he dipped his pen in human suffering to write his infamous "Mein Kamphital!" Marxistism is not, however, our only foe. The biggest threat exists here at home from those who spout the Constitution and the Bill of Rights, as though they owned them, for the purpose of aiding and abetting the malcontents who are sworn to destroy those very instruments. Firemen fighting for the rights of arsonists. These misguided dupes, as cancerous as any Communist cell, have permanated every level of our society. [*Moving forward, menacingly*] But, rest assured, this country will be saved in spite of its priciples! Mastergate was not the last operation I set in motion. Not by a long shot. Keep reading your morning headlines. Watch your nightly news. It's only a matter of time before you're "scandalized" by the stars of the next, inevitable Whatever-Gate: another crowd of photo-opportunistic nobodies who grab the limelight before either being sent on to jail or up to higher office! [*A pause*] This hearing is just one more episode in a series that will never end. [*Taking a remote TV channel changer from his pocket*] You will convene no further, Mr. Chairman.

MERRY CHASE: [*In the darkness*] You're watching live, the dead Mr. Slaughter.

SLAUGHTER: Until next time, this Committee —

> *He holds the channel changer above his head and clicks it. The overhead lights go off, with an accompanying sound effect that repeats throughout the fol-*

lowing. Pointing the changer at one end of the Committee's table.

You!

He clicks the changer. The lights go down on those Committee Members. He points the changer at the other end of the Committee table.

And you!

He clicks the changer. The balance of the Committee is plunged into darkness. Aiming the changer at the audience:

And you! [*Beat*] You're *all* adjourned!

He clicks the changer — and darkness envelops us all.

THE END

POSTSCRIPT

MERRY CHASE — Has her own network political talk show, "60 Seconds." Once a week, for one minute, national and international leaders meet with Ms. Chase to assess, discuss and diagnose cures for the most pressing problems of the world.

SENATOR BOWMAN — Resigned from office under a cloud of shame and embarrassment when it was revealed that not one member of his family was on his payroll.

CONGRESSMAN PROCTOR — Defeated by a much younger opponent after his 60 years of service in the Congress, Proctor retired gracefully, but still shows up every day for roll call.

SENATOR BUNTING — Narrowly escaped impeachment after he was discovered in the Senate cloak room, where he and two Pages were found stuck together.

CONGRESSMAN BYERS — Presently serving five years in prison for falsifying his income tax returns. Byers claimed that his costly drug habit justified naming himself as a dependent.

SENATOR KNIGHT — Facing charges of accepting kickbacks from defense contractors disguised as campaign funds.

CONGRESSMAN SELLERS — Facing charges of blackmailing Senator Knight, disguising the funds as kickbacks from defense contractors.

SHEPHERD HUNTER — Picked by the Committee for his clean-cut good looks, Hunter's services are now in such great demand that he hardly has time to complete his law studies.

VICE PRESIDENT BURDEN — Found guilty of lying to both houses of Congress, the OAS, NATO and the UN, Burden went on to be elected President. Once in that office, he granted himself a complete pardon.

SECRETARY OF STATE BISHOP — Has returned to the private sector as consultant to the heads of the Arab League, where his impersonations of Israeli politicians has them rolling on the rugs.

STEWARD BUTLER — Painfully aware of how bumbling and inept he had appeared on national television, Butler tried to take his life. He quit after the fourth attempt.

ABEL LAMB — Forswearing any further government involvement, Lamb went back to night classes in mathematics and bookkeeping. He is now a born again accountant.

MAJOR BATTLE — At his subsequent trial, the Major was charged with perjuring himself before the Committee, for contempt of Congress and for obstructing justice by wrongfully altering and destroying government documents. Found guilty on all counts, he is presently touring high schools and lecturing the young, in line with his being sentenced to serve 1,500 hours as a role model.

WYLIE SLAUGHTER — Now on the lecture circuit, where his remains command up to $50,000 an appearance. (A handshake is $5,000 more.)

POWER FAILURE

Power Failure was originally produced by the American Repertory Theatre, Cambridge, Massachusetts, with the following cast:

Will ....Christopher Lloyd

Coyne ....Christine Estabrook

Billings ....David Margulies

Worth ....Jeremy Geidt

Snow ....Christopher Lloyd

Myra ....Candy Buckley

Armor..David Margulies

Graves...Christopher Lloyd

Keene ....Christine Estabrook

Little ....Thomas Derrah

Directed by Michael Engler
Set by Philipp Jung
Costumes by Candice Donnelly
Lighting by Natasha Katz
Projections by Wendall K. Harrington
Sound by Maribeth Back

Scene 1. *Death Row*
WILL, a convict
COYNE, an author

Scene 2. *A Dressing Room*
COYNE
BILLINGS, her husband, a physician

Scene 3. *A Medical Office*
BILLINGS
WORTH, a man of wealth

Scene 4. *The Justice Department*
WORTH
SNOW, a government prosecutor

Scene 5. *A Room Somewhere*
SNOW
MYRA, a woman for hire

Scene 6. *A Bedroom*
MYRA
ARMOR, a defense contractor

Scene 7. *A Golf Course*
ARMOR
GRAVES, of the Pentagon

Scene 8. *A Dump Site*
GRAVES
KEENE, a congresswoman

Scene 9. *A Rectory*
KEENE
LITTLE, a man of the cloth

Scene 10. *Death Row*
LITTLE
WILL

The action takes place in various cities,

over a period of several months.

Scene 1 — Death Row

Present are WILL, *in convict's garb, and* COYNE, *a plainly-dressed author. There is a small tape recorder on the table between them. After a long pause:*

COYNE: Tell me, Will. [*Getting no response*] You said you would. [*Still none*] Will?

WILL [*Sullenly*]: I heard you.

COYNE: I need to —

WILL [*Cuts in*]: I'm not in the next room, in case you didn't notice.

COYNE: I need to get it down on tape, you know that. I want to get it exactly right.

WILL: I'll be in there soon enough. Way soon enough, oh, yeah.

COYNE: Maybe not.

WILL: Don't give me that. I'm all out of maybe's. And maybe-nots, for sure.

COYNE: I'm trying to make a difference, Will.

WILL: You are, huh?

COYNE: You know I am. You don't have to ask.

WILL: You got some problem with it, if I do?

COYNE [*Wearily*]: Do we have to go through this every time? Why?

WILL: That was *my* question. You're one why behind, okay?

COYNE [*A beat*]: Because I believe you, Will. [*Locking eyes*] Because I believe in you.

> [*After staring at her for a long moment, he nods at the recorder*]

WILL: Turn it on.

COYNE: It is. It's on.

WILL [*Leaning toward it*]: One, two, three, testing. One, two, three, testing.

COYNE: It's working.

WILL: Play it back.

COYNE: You haven't said anything.

WILL: What I just did. Play what I said back. I want to hear me, while I still can.

COYNE: Hold on.

[*She pushes the right buttons. From the recorder:*]

WILL'S VOICE: "One, two, three, testing. One, two, three, testing."

COYNE'S VOICE: "It's on."

WILL'S VOICE: "Play it back."

COYNE'S VOICE: "You haven't said anything."

COYNE [*Resetting the tape*]: Okay? You ready?

[*He suddenly seems miles away*]

Will?

WILL: You know what's in there? In the next room? In the room? Nothing. It's like a box. Just one box away from the last one. No windows. Just four sides of nothing. Not a stick of furniture. Furniture's for sitting around, talking. There's nothing in there till they open the door and roll in the gurney. They've got to have the gurney. They've got to give you wheels. There's no walking out. Not after they lay you down. Lay you down and strap you in.

COYNE: Will...

WILL: Did you know they use safety belts? Three of them. Chest, legs, feet. Not for you, though. To protect them. So they don't get hurt because you'd be bouncing off the walls if they didn't tie you down. And then, after they fasten them. After everybody's all nice and safe—[*Puts his hands on his own head, then cocks his ear*] You hear that?

COYNE: What?

WILL: You didn't hear that noise?

COYNE: I don't hear anything. [*Inching the recorder toward him*] Will?

WILL [*A beat, then*]: The injection, it's like a kind of immunization. Just one shot and there's no way you can ever get anything after that. Nothing. No cancer. No AIDS, whatever. You name it, I'm going to be safe. No pain. No feeling bad. No feeling good. No feeling. It's just one shot. They stuff you in a Glad bag. Over and out. [*Alarmed*] Jesus, that noise is my heart!

COYNE [*Patiently*]: Will? You promised you'd talk about it today. You said you'd tell me the dream.

WILL [*Impatiently*]: It's in the trial stuff. It was in all the papers.

COYNE: I want it in your voice. I want the feelings behind the words. I need to be able to play it back whenever I need to.

WILL: *Need* to? My God, why would anybody *need* to? I'd give anything not to know it. Anything if I could rewind my mind. Erase that part, make it blank. Jesus, what I wouldn't give to go back and undream the whole thing.

COYNE: Tell it to me, Will. Tell me the dream. [*She moves the tape recorder closer to him*]

WILL: Starts out, I'm sleeping. I don't mean I'm sleeping and I'm having a dream, 'cause there's no doing one without the other.

[*A beat, then:*]

COYNE [*Getting him on track*]: So, in your dream, you're sleeping.

WILL: Right. And in *that*, in *there*, is where the dream is. You know what I'm saying?

COYNE: That you were two dreams away from reality.

WILL: Exactly, yeah. That I was twice removed from what happened.

COYNE: Even though what you dreamed is very much what might have actually occurred. That your dream might be the only account of it.

WILL: Even though, yeah. But dreaming and doing are two completely different ball games. I mean, there's lots that I wouldn't dream of doing that I've sometimes dreamt that I did.

COYNE: But in this particular dream...

WILL: There's a mouth. [*He stops*]

COYNE: Tell me about it. Tell me about the mouth.

WILL: It's big as the room. It's foul, it's filthy. It's a toilet. Bright red, it is. Not just the lips. The teeth, too. Red lips. Red tongue. Red teeth. Like fangs. It pulls back the covers. It's all quiet. It licks all around. It bites, it grinds. It chews up her flesh and spits out the bones. First, her thumb. Then, her pinkie. Then, everything in between, till finally Marilyn's left hand's completely gone. Except for her wedding ring. It's like her hand is like a snack. Like ladyfingers. Then, the heavy stuff really starts. There's ripping and tearing. Whole sections go. That's when it hits him. That's when the realization sinks in.

> [*Silence. Until:*]

COYNE: That what, Will? What?

WILL: That her heart is still beating.

COYNE: She's still alive?

WILL: Right. After all that's happened, her heart just doesn't know any better.

> [*Her look implores him to continue*]

He has to kill her.

COYNE: *He* does, Will? A man did all that?

WILL: A man's mouth.

COYNE: Who is he, Will? Do you know him?

WILL: I only know his voice. Inside my head.

COYNE: And how does he do it, then? How does he kill Marilyn?

WILL: You know.

COYNE: *You* tell me.

WILL [*A beat, then*]: He brings Hope down on her head.

COYNE: Hope was your five year old.

WILL: One day short. The birthday cake was in the refrigerator. [*A beat*] He never touched any of that. Didn't want any of her cake. [*Another beat*] Just her shoulder. Bit it straight through.

COYNE: Like he did Debbie's arm.

WILL [*Correcting her*]: *Navel.*

COYNE: Sorry.

WILL: Nice try.

COYNE: What do you mean?

WILL: Good going.

COYNE [*Confused*]: Will?

WILL: You're not trying to trip me up, right?

COYNE: Why would I want to do that?

WILL: You'd be the first one who didn't.

COYNE: Will, why am I writing this book? Have you forgotten?

WILL: It gets pretty hard to remember when you try to catch me like that, I can tell you.

COYNE: I didn't. I never have. That's not what I'm about. You are no more a murderer than I am. You're a kind, caring person, who is caught up, literally, in a nightmare. I believe in your innocence. Totally. If I do my job right, so will everyone else in the world, when the book comes out.

WILL: Stick a copy in the Glad bag.

COYNE: Not if we move fast.

WILL: You really think?

COYNE: We've got two months before — [*She nods in the direction of the other room*] My publisher promised we can be in the stores before then.

WILL: But we can go for some of the other things before then, can't we? That we talked about? Like the movie sale?

COYNE: Sure, of course. We can peddle the manuscript, once I've got one.

WILL: You can send it to the studios?

COYNE: Right.

WILL: We can do that soon?

COYNE: As soon as you give me what I need on tape.

WILL: I know who it should be, if he only would.

COYNE: Who should be who, Will?

WILL: Who should be me. In the movie. Don't laugh. I know it's a wild shot. Tom Hanks. I know he does mostly comedy, but he's very wholesome. There's a whole innocent thing about him. You understand what I'm saying? His innocence would sort of attach itself to mine. Together, Tom and I would make a very powerful statement. I wish you'd write that down. Tom Hanks.

COYNE: It'll be on the tape.

WILL: Right. [*To the recorder*] Tom Hanks.

COYNE: Can we get back to the dream, Will?

WILL: There's a sweetness about him, too, you know? Tom? [*A beat, then*] Where was I, you remember?

COYNE: Debbie's navel.

WILL [*Remembering*]: You're not the only one's tried to trip me up. The truth's the truth, I can only tell it one way.

COYNE: You did fail your polygraph test, Will. It's in the police records.

WILL [*Scornfully*]: The police. Where were the police when Marilyn's head was rolled under the bed like some bowling ball with its eyes still open? Where were they, at some Winchells', having doughnuts when my babies were mauled and mangled and bashed against the wall? [*A beat, then*] Wait a minute! Jesus, why didn't I think of it before?! What about De Niro? De Niro for me instead of Tom Hanks.

COYNE: I'm not sure.

WILL: He's awful good.

COYNE: He's played a lot of heavies.

WILL: That's true. He was Godfather Two, wasn't he?

COYNE: And Al Capone. And Jake La Motta.

WILL: Yeah, right, I forgot. God, I hated when he kept hitting his wife. If we got De Niro I'd run the risk of the audience thinking I was guilty right from the start, is that what you're thinking?

COYNE: Right.

WILL: I agree with you. Yeah. Yeah. Yeah, sure, yeah. Yeah. [*Another emotional shift*] Y'know, sometimes...

COYNE: Yes?

WILL: I have to know this, okay? Once and for all, I just do, instead of just taking my own word for it.

COYNE: What, Will? Tell me.

WILL: I really didn't do it, did I? What I'm going to die for doing, if I did?

COYNE: Why do you say that?

WILL: I don't know. There's just some part of me never stops asking. I mean, if I didn't do it, then why did I dream it exactly the way they said it happened?

COYNE: You have any idea?

WILL: I think because they've taken my dream and said that's what happened because that's all they had to go on. But I couldn't have done what they said I did. Not to my girls. Not to all my girls.

COYNE: Will, listen to me.

WILL: Yes.

COYNE: There is not a fiber in either my private or

professional being that doesn't believe that you are completely innocent. Do you understand that?

WILL: I need to. I really need to.

COYNE: Do you understand that I simply couldn't make the emotional investment in you that I've made if I didn't feel — sense — *know* — that every word you've told me is true. In my mind's eye, I stare at the same walls your daughters were hurled against. I stare and I share the same sense of horror and disbelief that I know tortures you every single minute of the day.

WILL: You talk and I hear my own heart, do you know that? Oh, God, those walls. Those walls, covered with my children. My babies.

> [*He extends a hand toward hers. She doesn't take it, but rather turns hers to check her watch*]

Is that it for today?

COYNE: I'm afraid so. [*She turns off the tape recorder*]

WILL: You help me, y'know. Whatever happens, I can never thank you enough. I look at you and see Marilyn.

> [COYNE, *not all that comfortable with the compliment, rises*]

Wait. Before you go...

COYNE [*Turning on the tape recorder once more*]: Yes?

WILL [*A beat, then*]: Is there a chance — just a prayer
— we could get Tom Cruise?

   [*Lights down*]

Scene 2 — A Dressing Room

> BILLINGS, *in tuxedo trousers and underwear, gets into a dress shirt, cuff links and black tie. He will finish dressing throughout the scene.*

BILLINGS [*Annoyed, to someone Offstage*]: I just wish to hell you'd asked me before you accepted.

WOMAN'S VOICE [*Offstage*]: What?

BILLINGS [*Louder*]: I said I wish you'd have asked me before you accepted. You'd have a shit fit if I did this to you.

WOMAN'S VOICE [*Offstage*]: Darling, I did ask you. Two weeks ago.

BILLINGS: What?

WOMAN'S VOICE [*Offstage*]: I did, two weeks ago.

BILLINGS: Not me, you didn't. You've got me mixed up with some other husband.

WOMAN'S VOICE [*Offstage*]: We definitely discussed whether or not you wanted to go.

BILLINGS: And I said yes?

WOMAN'S VOICE [*Offstage*]: You said no.

BILLINGS [*Only half amused*]: Well, as long as I didn't agree to it.

[*The woman enters. It is* COYNE, *wearing an elegant dressing gown*]

COYNE: We said we'd go but we didn't have to stay.

BILLINGS: How about if we stay just long enough to leave?

COYNE: It's my last chance to see Verity before she goes to Paris.

[*As she applies make-up, deodorant and finishes dressing:*]

BILLINGS: Fine, okay, as long as you don't mind people thinking you've shown up with your late husband.

COYNE: *Somebody* in this room had a rough day.

BILLINGS: The hospital was a certifiable madhouse.

COYNE: Poor darling.

BILLINGS: I must have seen a hundred patients. More. I lost count.

COYNE: You said you were going to cut down.

BILLINGS: I can't really help myself once I get there. Or rather, once they do. It exhausts me.

COYNE: That's the price you pay for being such a dedicated, medical corporation.

[*As they continue their preparations:*]

BILLINGS [*Sighs*]: God, I need this evening like a second rectum.

COYNE: No shop talk, please.

BILLINGS [*Resigned*]: Only for you.

COYNE: You're an angel.

BILLINGS: You're just a proud owner.

COYNE: And you're my sanity. In a time when it seems as though someone's taken out a contract on the world, you are my rock of reasonableness, my bridge to decency.

BILLINGS: Here's a message from the bridge, okay? This is Captain Decent talking. Ten o'clock, we leave. You got that? Not one penny later. Not one bore more.

COYNE: Ten o'clock. You got it. Unless —

BILLINGS [*Cutting in*]: Don't unless me.

COYNE: *Unless* you find yourself actually having a good time. It can't really hurt you to spend some time with people who've got their clothes on once in awhile, can it?

BILLINGS: You have some kind of idea that being around nudity constantly is a picnic? You think that physicians like looking at lumps and bumps? That we fancy folds, that we're connoisseurs of creases?

COYNE: I can't imagine anything worse. I wouldn't be a mirror for all the money in the world.

> [BILLINGS *watches her study herself in the mirror a moment, then:*]

BILLINGS: You don't need much make-up tonight.

COYNE: You mind if I get a second opinion?

BILLINGS: Trust me. There's that extra blush in your cheeks you always get when you've been on Death Row.

COYNE: That comes from trying to scrape my skin off in the tub. [*Shudders*] He makes my flesh crawl. Ever spend an hour with someone and not inhale once?

BILLINGS: Was it worth it? Get any good stuff?

COYNE: It's an endless process. I literally have to pan for the truth. There's maybe one dram of it to every ton of his bullshit. The bastard is still lying through his teeth. I don't know what pisses me off more. The fact that he chewed halfway through his family or that he keeps underestimating my intelligence.

BILLINGS: Both capital crimes, of course.

COYNE: Today was the topper. Here's a guy tucks his kids in with an axe; the blood's barely dry on their Dr. Dentons and his big worry is who's going to play him in the movies.

BILLINGS: Really?

COYNE: I swear.

BILLINGS: I had no idea.

COYNE: I'm telling you.

BILLINGS: When did you make your picture deal?

COYNE: Sweetheart, don't ever say that again. You are never to repeat that phrase outside this room. Ever. To anyone. You are not to put the words "picture" and "deal" together in the same sentence, not even in the same paragraph, until after his execution. Verity made me swear I'd tell no one. The way she's set it up, Warner's is not going to sign my contract with them until after the word "dead" on Will's certificate, they write in "as a doornail." If he finds out about it now, if he even smells a hint of it, his agent is going to want all kinds of approvals for him. Credit. Some kind of profit participation. Who knows what kind of involvement? The truth is, once he butchered his family, his work was finished. Now, he's got to let go; let the rest of us get on with things. Being guilty of killing your wife and daughters doesn't automatically make someone an executive producer, you know, or a whole lot more people would be doing it.

BILLINGS: What if he's not? Have you thought of that?

COYNE: Not what? Guilty? Will? Are you serious?

BILLINGS: What if he's not executed?

COYNE: Bite your tongue.

BILLINGS: It happens.

COYNE: Not this time. Come the thirty-first of next month, at exactly seven a.m., Will starts hanging out with Ted Bundy.

BILLINGS: I hope so, for your sake.

COYNE: Sweetheart, not one scrap of new evidence has surfaced. No one else has come forward to confess.

BILLINGS: There's always clemency. He could get a call at six fifty-nine.

COYNE: Darling, where have you been? Don't you watch campaign commercials? Death is the flavor of the month.

BILLINGS: That's good. Write it down.

COYNE: I already have. You don't think I talk on spec, do you?

[*He smiles, kisses her forehead adoringly*]

Anyway, if public opinion *and* the trial transcripts *and* the police records aren't enough to keep the Governor's hand off the phone, there is some additional, very damning material that will convince her of Will's guilt unquestionably.

BILLINGS: There is such stuff?

COYNE: My notes. Stuff he never told anyone else. And a very detailed outline, the one I'm working from, that'll prove conclusively that it was Will, just Will, not some mysterious "him" who wiped out his family. It *is* all a dream, Will's *dream*. But first came the act and *then* came the dream. He made it a dream not so he could fool the state but so that he could go on living with himself. It's as though he's trying to sneak away from himself while he's not looking. And now, he's become this other person who's watching to see if who he really is is getting away with it. [*A beat, then*] I'm sounding as twisted as he is.

BILLINGS: I follow you.

COYNE: The man is guilty. I knew it before I met him. I went a whole day — as an experiment? — I went the whole day pretending he was innocent. My watch stopped. My pantyhose ran. I broke a nail. I couldn't fool my own ecosystem. It's all in my notes. My notes and my tapes, which I'm prepared to turn over if I detect even a hint of mercy.

BILLINGS: It would break his heart to know.

COYNE: You presuppose he has one. Any rate, he'll be long gone when the book comes out. [*Finishes dressing with a fanfare*] Ta daah!

BILLINGS: You look gorgeous.

COYNE: That's all?

BILLINGS [*Nibbling her hand*]: How about edible?

COYNE [*Withdrawing her hand*]: No ladyfingers, please. Shall we?

> [*Last minute stuff — collecting her bag, straightening his tie, etc. — when: The phone chirps — immediately triggering a sense of tension*]

COYNE: Shit!

BILLINGS [*Reassuringly*]: Maybe not.

> [*Another chirp*]

COYNE [*Losing it*]: It's him. It's that guy.

BILLINGS [*Dialing another phone*]: Don't pick it up!

COYNE: I really don't need this now.

> [*Chirp*]

Not today.

BILLINGS: Wait!

COYNE [*Wearily*]: I know, I know.

BILLINGS [*Into his phone*]: Sergeant Bates, please. Tell him it's Doctor Billings.

[*Chirp*]

BILLINGS [*Into his phone*]: Ken? [*Whispers, to* COYNE]: Got him.

[COYNE *removes one of her earrings and lifts the other receiver in mid-chirp*]

[*Into his phone, softly:*] We may be getting another one.

[COYNE *listens for a moment, then nods at* BILLINGS]

[*Into his receiver, softly:*] It's him.

COYNE [*After listening a bit more*]: Yes. I hear you.

[BILLINGS *checks his watch. Obviously, the longer her conversation goes on, the better*]

BILLINGS [*Into his receiver, anxiously*]: How you doing?

COYNE [*Listening, listening, then:*] Wait, wait! Hold it! Before you go, you listen to me a second, garbagemouth...

[BILLINGS *encourages her to go on talking*]

You make another of these one-handed calls, you ring this number just one more time to give your genitals a jump start and I'm going to run a chain saw through your groin and drape your private parts over one of your public phone booths. You understand? ... Yes, I *bet* you'd like that. What else would you like, as long as I've got you? ... Hello?

[*As she shrugs and hangs up:*]

BILLINGS [*Into his receiver*]: Yeah, he did. Just now ... Yeah, I figured. Right. Thanks. Hopefully, next time. Sorry, Ken. [*Hanging up*] He wasn't on long enough.

COYNE. On is not what that creep is trying to get.

BILLINGS: He knows just how much time he can spend. Probably times it to the second.

COYNE: Or the inch. Slimy bastard. [*Wiping her receiver with a Kleenex*] God, I need another bath. Which he's also offered to give me.

BILLINGS: Was that tonight's special?

COYNE: You know he never repeats himself. He's too creative for that. Let's go.

BILLINGS: I don't want you walking around with it all night.

COYNE [*A beat, then*]: I'm on my back. Naked.

BILLINGS: That's our boy.

COYNE: There's a satin sheet over me. Black. With one, round hole in it.

BILLINGS: In the sheet.

COYNE: About the size of a dinner plate, he said.

BILLINGS: That figures.

COYNE: Not that. He's got something for me. He's giving me a present. A pearl necklace. And I'm getting it one pearl at a time. Just telling it, he only got as far as the second pearl. [*She selects a strand of pearls from her jewel box, as he turns on the answering machine*] Don't turn it on.

BILLINGS: In case he leaves a message. For Bates.

COYNE: I've had enough sickness on tape for one day. [*Re pearls*] Help me.

BILLINGS: [*Standing behind her*] One pearl at a time, was that it?

COYNE: And not using his hands.

> [BILLINGS *lowers the pearls so that they trace her breasts*]

Darling ... [*Reminding him*]: It's nearly eight.

BILLINGS: ... Let's just see if we can't do one strand, shall we?

[*Lights down*]

Scene 3 — A Doctor's Office

WORTH *dressed in a Saville Row suit, waits anxiously. He checks his watch. He fidgets nervously with the seat of his pants, apparently ill at ease in them.* BILLINGS *enters, in a doctor's white jacket and a stethoscope around his neck, carrying a thick medical file.* WORTH *immediately takes his hand from his bottom, as though he has been caught at something.*

BILLINGS: Sorry to have taken so long.

WORTH: Quite all right.

BILLINGS: I wanted to double check everything.

WORTH: I understand.

BILLINGS: Each report. Very carefully.

WORTH: Of course. And?

BILLINGS: Perhaps you'd like to sit down?

WORTH: I'm fine.

BILLINGS: After running the most extensive, the most exhausting tests imaginable — [*Placing several x-rays on display*] Cardiovascular, respiratory, digestive system, neurological. The works. Every part of your body. I must tell you there is not a thing wrong with you, Mr. Worth.

WORTH: You're certain?

BILLINGS: You are totally sound. Remarkably so. I have patients who would die to be as healthy as you are, sir.

WORTH [*Staring at the x-rays*]: Absolutely nothing? I am perfectly fit?

BILLINGS: You could get a second opinion, of course. I think you'd find it largely a waste of time.

WORTH: Not my favorite word at the moment. Time.

DILLINGS: I assure you you have a good deal of it ahead you, sir, from a medical point of view.

WORTH: From a criminal point of view, I'm afraid I have even more.

BILLINGS: I won't be coy with you, Mr. Worth. I read the papers.

WORTH: I find it ironic, to say the least, that this country, which purports to be such a bastion of freedom should be so preoccupied with depriving me of my own. My lawyers have informed me that if I'm found guilty on only half the counts the government has charged me with, the minimum I can expect is five hundred years. Five hundred years, Doctor Billings. Half a millennium in a federal penitentiary.

BILLINGS: With no time off for — ?

WORTH: For good behavior? Yes, they tell me that could knock a century or so off my time. The fines, of course, will come to several hundred million. Conceivably a billion. It all depends on where the judge decides to put the comma.

BILLINGS: Well, trite as it may seem, you do still have your health.

WORTH: In truth, doctor, I find that a bit of a handicap right now.

BILLINGS: Oh?

WORTH: I won't be coy with you either. Doctor Billings, I would like you to do for me what you have on certain occasions done for others.

BILLINGS: My prescription pad is not for hire.

WORTH: I'm not interested in a prescription, sir. I want you to give me an illness. I want you to induce a disorder in me; create a designer disease that will make it difficult, if not impossible for me to appear in a court of law, but one that is, with proper treatment, reversible and, in any case, not in any way life threatening.

BILLINGS: And you're just assuming that I can, or would go, along with such a scheme?

WORTH: Doctors may not talk about their patients, doctor, but let me assure you that patients do a good deal of talking about their doctors.

BILLINGS: And do patients also talk about what the cost of such a procedure would come to?

WORTH: I know that it's seven figures, and that almost all of them are zeros.

BILLINGS: Mr. Worth, were such a treatment even remotely possible, I imagine it would be necessary to engage the assistance of a number of other people. In addition to having to perform certain — how to put it? — unique applications of medicine — they would need a considerable amount of coaching. They would be required to say what they were told to say at the appropriate time.

WORTH: Of course.

BILLINGS: There are others who would be required to say nothing at all. That kind of silence could be golden and a half.

WORTH: Going to eight figures would be no problem at all. If you could see the world as I have seen it, you would know that outrageous has no meaning for me.

BILLINGS [*Into his intercom*]: Helen, please hold all calls. [*An added thought*] Oh, if it's an emergency, say I'm out of town. [*To* WORTH] Please sit down.

WORTH: I prefer to stand.

BILLINGS: Given your requirements, sir, there are several options I believe are possible, each of which I can guarantee will diminish your health in varying degrees.

WORTH: You *can* make me ill?

BILLINGS: I can.

WORTH: You're certain?

BILLINGS: I'd stake my reputation as a doctor on it, sir. The possibilities available cover a range of severity.

WORTH: Not too severe, I would hope.

BILLINGS: The choice has a good deal to do with the PR factor. During the course of the illness, the public would be treated to a steady stream of pictures and footage of you in a variety of telegenically sympathetic situations. You, on a stretcher. Or in an ambulance. Or seen on various life-support systems. Medical teams rushing from choppers to vans with organ transplants, if that is the route we decide to go.

WORTH: There is a history of phlebitis in my family, if that helps me at all.

BILLINGS: Phlebitis.

WORTH: Isn't that what you gave to Nixon?

BILLINGS: It was a rather obvious choice. By the time I saw him, the man literally didn't have a leg to stand on. I, more or less, made the metaphor medical. But I'm not sure it's a good idea to repeat myself. Are you familiar with endocarditis? [WORTH *is not*] It's an inflammation of the membrane that lines the heart. Sounds like passion, actually it's pus. I could give it to you quite simply by causing a bacterial infection.

WORTH: Sounds a bit drastic.

BILLINGS: It happens routinely in hospitals. Only here, I'm admitting it.

WORTH: What precisely would I be letting myself in for?

BILLINGS: You would display certain symptoms: fever, changes in heart rhythm that would be medically convincing to whichever doctors might be acting for the prosecution. Any damage to your heart valves, which I would hope to keep to a minimum, could be corrected by surgery later.

WORTH: You're certain?

BILLINGS: I had great success with that with Ferdinand Marcos.

WORTH: But he died, didn't he?

BILLINGS: An unfortunate side effect, to be sure. Perhaps there is a *cluster* of disorders we could whip together rather quickly. I could, with luck, give you all the symptoms of acrosyanosis, sometimes known as Raynaud's sign. It's an abnormal condition that is brought about by exposure to cold or emotional stress, both of which we could easily expose you to. You would take on a bluish coloration, which would, of course, photograph very well. I could implement this by giving you a condition known as dacryocystitus, inflaming your lacrimal or tear ducts which would cause continuous crying. As a last touch, you could be coached rather quickly to appear to be a victim of coprolalia. The La Tourette Syndrome? [WORTH *doesn't know it*] It manifests itself in a constant stream of uncontrollable grimaces, tics, grunts, in addition to compulsive outbursts of obscene and offensive remarks of the foulest nature. I think between the blue face and the blue language, with the tears thrown in for the sympathy factor, we'd have ourselves a very attractive package. I might just want to play around with a little anemia, too.

WORTH: You're the doctor. I'll take whatever you give me. With the exception of — I made a note of it — [*Checking a note in his pocket*] Tay-Sachs Disease. I'm advised that that's the only sickness I must positively stay clear of.

BILLINGS [*Taking the note from him*]: Have you been talking to someone about Tay-Sachs? You haven't been shopping around for other scenarios?

WORTH: No, no, it's just that my lawyers tell me that it is a disease that occurs almost exclusively among those of the Jewish faith.

BILLINGS: In young children, yes.

WORTH: You will appreciate that I do a great deal of business with Arab interests. While I'm sure they would quite enjoy the prospect of any Jew being unwell, especially a young one, I wouldn't want them to think that I'd been two-faced about my anti-Semitism.

BILLINGS: I understand.

WORTH: Well, then. When do we begin?

BILLINGS: Whatever we decide you're going to get, I think the sooner you see me, the better. Monday morning, if that's all right.

WORTH: Monday morning, I'm in Brussels. Perhaps you can join me on my plane? Could you do your work there?

BILLINGS: I might come along for the ride, just to talk further perhaps. I'd really rather infect you in the office, where everything's more sterile. If I start treating you, say, the following Monday, I think, with any luck, I can have you on your back within a week.

WORTH: It's essential that I attend my daughter's wedding on the twentieth.

BILLINGS: We'll get you there somehow. I read that

Father Little will be performing the ceremony?

WORTH: It can't hurt at this particular time for me to be seen standing beside a man of his stature on the six o'clock news.

BILLINGS: Quite.

WORTH: Before I go, perhaps we should nail down the precise fee?

BILLINGS: I always prefer to do it on the first visit. Shall we say, ten million plus any out-of-pocket expenses?

WORTH: And what sort of payment do you prefer?

BILLINGS: I'm rather neutral about it. Switzerland will be fine.

WORTH: I took the liberty of opening a bank account in Zurich that would supply the funds for your services in this matter. All that remains is for you and I to agree upon a password so that you may draw your fee from the amount on deposit immediately. This is the bank book.

BILLINGS: Thank you.

WORTH: And I believe I have the ideal password, if you agree.

BILLINGS [*Helping him into his topcoat*]: Yes?

WORTH: May I suggest "Hippocrates"?

BILLINGS [*Smiles*]: Perfect.

> [*As* BILLINGS *opens the door for him,* WORTH *once more tugs at the back of his trousers. Then, using the same hand to shake* BILLINGS':]

WORTH: Good day, sir.

BILLINGS: Good day to you.

> [*And* WORTH *is out the door. Blackout*]

Scene 4 — The Justice Department

SNOW *sits at his desk, a small tape recorder to his ear.* WORTH *sits, waiting.*

WORTH'S VOICE [*Over, on tape*]: "You *can* make me ill?"

BILLINGS' VOICE [*Same*] "I can."

WORTH'S VOICE: "You're certain?"

BILLINGS' VOICE: "I'd stake my reputation as a doctor on it, sir."

[SNOW *fast forwards the recorder*]

WORTH'S VOICE: "Perhaps we should nail down the precise fee?"

BILLINGS' VOICE: "I always prefer to do it on the first visit. Shall we say, ten million plus any out-of-pocket expenses?"

SNOW [*Gleefully*]: Got him! Got him stone cold! We've finally nailed the son-of-a-bitch! Let me be more accurate. You nailed him!

WORTH: I merely carried out my side of our bargain.

SNOW: For years, I've been arresting this guy in my sleep. Never mind Nixon and Marcos and Martha

Mitchell. Ten minutes alone with Doctor Billings and Jack Ruby suddenly gets cancer. One house call and William Casey's head cold turns into a brain tumor. A real pistol, the good doctor. Definitely the man to see if you wanted to give someone a gift death certificate. The Justice Department is grateful to you, sir.

WORTH [*Shrugs*]: As I said.

SNOW: We appreciate your accepting the special conditions this particular situation involved.

WORTH: It should come as no surprise to you, Mr. Snow, the lengths to which I'd go to avoid spending even one day less than the five hundred years in prison you have in mind for me.

SNOW: We hope to capitalize on that feeling, sir, to the mutual benefit of you and the government. [*Taking the tiny cassette from the recorder*] This is going to help change how you spend your time considerably. The same may be said of Dr.Billings, as well.

[WORTH *rises, adjusts the seat of his pants slightly*]

Second thoughts, Mr. Worth?

WORTH: Not at all. I'm afraid I'm not entirely over the effects of the recording device your people planted on me.

SNOW: They tell me you were somewhat annoyed, our not providing you with a more standard wire.

WORTH: I confess to a certain amount of discomfort. When you broached the idea, I assumed I would simply be wearing a small microphone across my chest.

SNOW: Thing was, we just couldn't risk blowing the entire operation in case Billings asked you to remove your shirt for some reason or other.

WORTH: I understand.

SNOW: I apologize for any uneasiness it may have caused you.

WORTH: I was fine, providing I didn't sit down. Tell me, have you used this particular piece of equipment before?

SNOW: Actually, you're the first to try it. We'd be very interested in your comments. We're anxious to make it function better, if we can.

WORTH: I should tell you that since it's voice-activated, I received a slight shock every time Dr. Billings began to speak.

SNOW: A shock?

WORTH: A twinge.

SNOW: Painful?

WORTH: At first. Surprisingly, I soon found myself hanging on his every word.

[SNOW *laughs, makes some notes*]

SNOW: Gotcha. Our plans call for you to wear a somewhat different set-up at your daughter's wedding. [*Unbuttoning his vest*] Do you mind?

WORTH: Different recording apparatus?

SNOW: Right.

WORTH: You're suggesting I be wired at my own daughter's wedding?

SNOW: It's your call to make, Mr. Worth. Like you, we want to do all we can to reduce your sentence. [*Sensing* WORTH's *reluctance*] For all your power, Mr. Worth; for all that you are in the world, it wouldn't take long in prison for a man of your position to find himself in a few he never dreamt of. Three or four nights, a week at the most, of being passed around, and I promise you'll feel like a very tired, very soiled rag doll.

WORTH: What sort of apparatus?

SNOW [*Loosening his tie*]: The department feels that with all the inevitable hugging that will be going on the big day, all the body contact, we wouldn't want to take a chance on anyone feeling a recorder strapped anywhere on you. [*Hands him a business card*] We can take care of that Wednesday morning, ten o'clock.

WORTH: Dr. Braun? He's a dentist?

SNOW: Right. Dr. Braun will implant a bug under one of your existing crowns. It's a micro-mike, about the size of a raspberry pip. When it's firmly in there, anyone talking within five feet of your mouth will be transmitting directly to our location in one of the catering vans outside your estate. [*Handing him a clipboard, with several sheets of paper attached*] Let's look at the guest list, shall we?

> [WORTH *takes a pair of reading glasses from a case. Before he can put them on,* SNOW *reaches for them*]

May I? [SNOW *takes the glasses from him, looks them over carefully*]

WORTH: You're not serious? You think I would secretly tape our conversation about the conversations you want me to secretly tape?

SNOW: Let me tell you, Mr. Worth, the one lesson you learn the longer you work here at Justice. There is none. We've had enough sure-fire cases shot out from under us to teach us that trust is just a word we use to help fill up the space on money.

> [*He returns the glasses, to* WORTH, *who puts them on and studies the paper with great deliberation.* SNOW *checks his watch, impatiently, then:*]

What do you think? Who would you like to start with?

> [*As* WORTH *stares at the list*]

You'll notice a number beside each name. That figure represents the length of time I believe I can put that person away, based on your cooperation in getting them to spill their guts. Which time would be deducted from your own.

WORTH: I understand. [*A beat, then*] Let's start with my father.

SNOW: A touching choice.

WORTH: What do you need to know?

SNOW: We'd like you to get him to talk about Olympus Insurance. Specifically, if you could discuss in detail what the two of you did with the quarter of a billion dollars you withheld in claims from the company's policy holders.

WORTH: That's already been well-documented.

SNOW: Your role in it has, yes. We want what will amount to a full confession from your father. From his lips, right to your own, so to speak.

WORTH: You understand that it's difficult for him to communicate, since his stroke.

SNOW: Be patient, just give him your loving attention. We'll do the same. We'd especially like to know about the amount of interest that quarter of a billion is generating in the off shore accounts he secretly set up for the purpose of laundering the money.

WORTH [*Re list*]: If convicted, my father's sentence would be between eighty and a hundred years?

SNOW: In view of your conscientiousness, I would, of course, go for the higher figure.

WORTH: I'll just pencil in ninety. [*He does that, then further consults the list*] You have my two brothers down here.

SNOW: In connection with the Sand L scam that put five hundred million dollars in your pockets.

WORTH: Of course. [*Frowning*] They're grouped with my oldest son.

SNOW: In view of the fact that they helped screw your investors out of half a bill, you'll see that they stand to do a hundred years each. Their three hundred plus your father's ninety and you begin to see a little daylight, huh?

WORTH: I would think if you were able to convict all three that would be worth a little something extra, would it not?

SNOW: I guess if you can bowl a strike, I might be able to get you a ten percent bonus. How does another thirty years off hit you?

WORTH: Why don't we round it off to fifty?

SNOW: I guess we're really talking forty. [*Using a*

handkerchief to wipe his brow] Either way, if we're using the same numbers, we've whittled your own sentence down to under a hundred years. [*Re list*] You make the right choices there and you could be just about home free. Half a dozen more conversations could do the trick.

> [*As* WORTH *studies the list,* SNOW *again checks his watch, chews at his thumbnail*]

WORTH: My wife is worth fifty years?

SNOW: Your daughter, sixty.

WORTH: I'm not sure how much time I'm going to be alone with her on this particular occasion. It is her wedding day.

SNOW: You only need three, four minutes together, tops.

WORTH: You only want to hear about the drugs she's brought into the country on our plane? Is that it?

SNOW: To the nearest ton.

WORTH: I can get you the yacht figures from my wife.

SNOW: We'd love that.

WORTH [*Jots on the paper, then*]: Her fifty year sentence, plus my daughter's sixty, would put me over the top, would it not? Over the wall, I suppose, is more like it.

SNOW: It would, indeed. However, Mrs. Worth could prove a bit more difficult than the others to deal with. Her attorneys are preparing for her own upcoming trial. In that connection, I should warn you that we've discovered that Mrs. Worth will also be wearing a wire at the wedding. Therefore, you're going to have to be extremely careful, since you and your wife will be bugging each other.

WORTH: You don't think she'll assume that I'm wired, too?

SNOW: Incriminate yourself. Say too much. It might encourage her to say just a little.

WORTH: And give her attorneys that ammunition?

SNOW: She won't tape so much as a syllable. [On WORTH's *quizzical look*] There'll be a jamming device in your ear.[WORTH *raises his eyebrows*] Your *ear*. It will affect only her system, not yours. You just have to be sure not to embrace her when she speaks.

WORTH: Nothing she says can be held against me?

SNOW: Exactly. You realize, Mr. Worth, that if I'm able to convict your wife — [*Using his pocket calculator:*] The only thing the judge may give you is a ticket for speeding through court.

WORTH: There is still the matter of the fine, of course.

SNOW [*Getting his topcoat and* WORTH'*s*]: I would say

that, given the extent of your cooperation with the government, I can almost promise to get that down to under ten figures.

WORTH: In any case, all tax deductible.

SNOW: Exactly. [*He dumps* WORTH's *topcoat on the man*]

WORTH: I take it we're finished.

SNOW: If you'll just initial that list.

    [WORTH *complies.* SNOW *tears off the top sheet*]

Your copy.

WORTH: Thank you. [*As* SNOW *hustles him to the door*] I don't want to get caught in Friday traffic.

SNOW [*Opening the door*]: I've got to run myself.

WORTH: I couldn't help noticing. [*As* SNOW *opens the door:*] Friday is the one day of the week I really hate to be late. [*Re list*] We all so look forward to sitting down to family dinner. [*He exits*]

    [SNOW *immediately, hurriedly starts to jam some of his paper work into an attache case. He stops as his intercom buzzes. Dashing to it, he picks up the receiver*]

SNOW [*Into intercom, annoyed*]: Yes? ... Cancel 'em ... I know, but I can't ... If we lose 'em, we lose 'em, that's all! [*Suddenly cowering, as though he sees something menacing on the ceiling; then, into intercom*] I've got to go!

[*He goes to a filing cabinet, takes out a brown paper bag and stuffs it into the attache case, acting all the while as though He is being watched. Finished packing, He goes to the door and turns out the light at the wall, as He exits. A beat, and the door reopens quickly.* SNOW *steps back into the room and turns the light on again. To the empty room, with a mad look:*]

Think I don't know you're here, huh?

[*The lights fade*]

Scene 5 — A Room Somewhere

MYRA *is discovered, her loose wrap allowing us glimpses of the pale flesh beneath. Taking a new, floral scarf from a department store shopping bag, she uses the audience as a mirror, draping the scarf over her shoulder, this way and that, looking for the best effect. The phone warbles.*

MYRA [*Answering it*]: Hello? ... Merrilee? ... Anything wrong? ... Okay, so he's ten minutes late. [*With authority*] You just wait in the lobby where you're supposed to. The john'll be there. I've already put the charge on his Visa card ... Don't worry about looking conspicuous ... Sweetie, you are not going to get busted. None of my girls are. Not in this town. Ever. Listen, I've got my own gig to do, baby. I'll check with you later.

[*She hangs up. Putting the scarf into her shopping bag, she takes drug paraphernalia out of it — a glass pipe, vial, cigarette lighter, etc. She is heating the vial, preparing a mixture, as the door buzzer sounds*]

Yes?

[*The buzzer is heard again. One long, a pause, then two short.* MYRA, *goes to the door to admit her caller,* SNOW, *his attache case in hand. He enters, filled with paranoia, light years away from the cool*] *professional who began the previous scene*]

SNOW: There was one in the hall! [*Closing the door quickly*] I saw him! He thought I didn't, but I did!

MYRA: You didn't see anybody.

SNOW: That doesn't mean they weren't there!

MYRA: Trust me. You need a key to get in.

SNOW: There never was one key that didn't become another one. I saw him!

MYRA: You saw no one. You're just running on empty.

[*As he puts his case down and looks cautiously through the curtain windows:*]

SNOW [*Re drug preparations*]: How we doing?

MYRA: Almost.

SNOW: I thought it'd be ready.

MYRA: You're early.

SNOW: I didn't want to be late.

MYRA: In a minute.

SNOW: No such thing. Minutes are bullshit. They're just hours broken up into little pieces.

MYRA: Come on, now. Easy, willya?

SNOW: Easy's easy for you to say. I just let two Nazis off the hook, so I could get here. I had their fingerprints on corpses and I let them take a cab.

MYRA: Okay, okay. You want to settle up for everything now? Save you the trouble later?

[SNOW *takes several bills from his wallet.* MYRA *tucks them into her panties*]

That's a good baby. Let me get you your nummies.

[*She returns to her labors, as* SNOW *removes his jacket and tie*]

Somebody's had a rough day at the office.

SNOW: It never stops. Never. Justice is not only blind. It's exhausting. Fucking civil rights. Equal rights. Human rights. Nobody ever settles for two out of three. [*A beat, then*] So?

MYRA: Just about.

SNOW [*Opening his attache case*]: I got some for tomorrow.

MYRA [*Reminding him*]: The day after.

SNOW: Jesus, you really won't be here?

MYRA: Only for the day.

SNOW: You can't do that to me. Can't you get out of it?

MYRA: I told you. I have to.

SNOW: You want to. You just want to get away.

MYRA: Nothing wrong with that.

SNOW: Bullshit. If being out of town wasn't somewhere else, believe me, no one'd ever go there.

> [*Removing the paper bag, he takes a bag of cocaine from it*]

MYRA [*Smiles*]: Sure you got enough?

SNOW: Pure. Hasn't been stepped on. Judge Holden brought it back from Columbia. You're looking at some prime Exhibit "A."

MYRA: Great.

> [*Pacing anxiously,* SNOW *takes another peek through the curtains and quickly steps back*]

SNOW: Seeing things, huh? Take a look for yourself! There's a cop in the tree!

MYRA [*Calmly*]: Sure, baby.

SNOW [*Taking another look*]: It's worse! He's FBI! I

know him! That's Nordstrum! FBI!

MYRA [*Patiently*]: Sweetie ...

SNOW: You think I don't know Nordstrum? After all the people we've framed together? [*Braving another peep out*] He's looking in! [*Cowering*] Oh, God, he sees me!

MYRA: There's nobody there.

SNOW: That's his cover. Being nobody.

MYRA: Okay, okay, but they can't see in. The shade is down.

SNOW: You think that stops them?

MYRA: Come on. Get real. The shade is down and there is no tree out there.

SNOW: You don't get it, do you? They bring their own! [*Digging into his attache case*] Where's that stapler?

MYRA: You think you can get them from here?

SNOW: Don't be a smartass. It's for the shade. [*At the window, he takes one more cautious peek out*] You were right. It's not Nordstrum. Nobody from the FBI glows in the dark like that.

MYRA: This guy glows in the dark?

SNOW: It's not a guy. It's one of the kids.

MYRA [*Playing along*]: The kind that glow?

SNOW: The ones who live downwind of the reactor.

MYRA: Which reactor?

SNOW: The one in Hanford, out in Washington. Don't play dumb with me. You think I don't know one when I see one? I'd know a downwinder in my sleep. I've seen all the pictures. I've seen them in person. The bulging throats. Eyeballs popping out of their sockets. The department sent me there often enough. Let me tell you one more time, and you pass it on to the rest of your shiny friends, okay? In case it still hasn't sunk in? You can sue what's left of your brains out, but no one, not you, not anyone else, is getting one dime from the U.S. government.

MYRA [*Playing along*]: I will, okay.

SNOW [*In terrible pain*]: God, are they ever going to go away? [*Confidentially*] I can tell *you*. Can you keep secret?

MYRA: There's nobody better.

SNOW: Okay. [*A beat*] There was a release of radioactivity. It's in their food. It's in their water.

MYRA: Accidents happen.

SNOW: Absolutely. Accidents happen. They happen all the time. It's an accident if an accident *doesn't* happen, right, babe?

MYRA: Right.

SNOW: You agree with me one more time, I'll put your head through the wall. [*A beat, then*] This was no accident, don't you understand? We released it on purpose. The government wanted to gauge the effect of radio-activity on the population.

MYRA: That can't be true.

SNOW: Are you going to tell me something we've been lying about for forty years isn't true?

MYRA [*In disbelief*]: The government? Our government?

SNOW: That's right. The good old U.S. of A. Contaminated mothers, fathers, little kids, whole families. Families who've got puppies with heads where their tails used to be! [*Re pipe*] When the fuck is that going to be ready?

MYRA [*Offering it to him*]: Hit it!

> [SNOW *grabs it eagerly, and takes a deep, deep drag. The effect of euphoria is immediate*]

SNOW: Oh, God! Oh, Jesus! Oh, oh, oh — oh, oh, oh, wow! Yes! Yes! Oh, wow! Listen! You hear that? That's my blood! Man, what a ride! What a rush! Come here! Come here! [*Pulling her to him*] Let me put my mouth where my money is! [*Kneeling before her, he presses his lips to her panties. Then, suddenly, abruptly, he pushes her away and snarls*] You're a slut! You don't have to go away tomorrow!

MYRA: It's just one day.

SNOW: Just one day? You know how many years of minutes there are in a day?! You got any idea what it's like to sit in a chair and watch your body climb the walls? Get 'em out! Go on, get 'em!

MYRA: So soon?

SNOW: Get 'em!

[*As* MYRA *digs into his attache case:*]

Get 'em out and put 'em on!

[MYRA *opens the case and takes out a pair of handcuffs*]

MYRA: *You* put them on me.

SNOW: Oh, no. No, no, no. I'm not making that kind of commitment.

[MYRA *puts the cuffs on her*]

Got 'em on? Good! Get out the tape!

[MYRA *takes a role of gaffer's tape from her*

shopping bag and hands it to him]

SNOW: You want this, don't you? You really want it?

MYRA: I don't have any choice, do I?

SNOW [*Re tape, angrily*]: Why didn't you cut it up? I've got to have strips, you know that. You know I need strips. You're no God damn good for anything, are you? [*Unrolling a length of tape, he bites off a strip, then:*] I tell you, it's a drag being totally all-powerful, when everybody else is just shit. What the hell are you staring at?! Sit down! You heard me! Sit!

> [MYRA *complies.* Humming grotesquely, SNOW *wraps the tape around her ankles*]

There we go!

> [MYRA *winces and shudders*]

Too tight?

MYRA: Yes.

SNOW: Perfect! [*Finished taping her*] Okay, now, kneel! Kneel! [*He forces her to her knees*]

MYRA [*"Frightened"*]: Don't kill me! Oh, God, don't kill me!

SNOW: You mean that, or are you just trying to please me? [*He reaches into his attache case and produces a leather mask*]

MYRA: What's that?!

SNOW: You're going to love it. [*Putting it on her*] It was my mother's. [*As she resists*] Stop squirming, God damn it! [*He finally gets the mask over her head. It covers everything but her mouth. Standing back, he stares at her in wonder and admiration*] God, you're beautiful when I'm angry!

[*And, as he starts to undo his belt: the lights fade*]

Scene 6 — A Bedroom

The bedside phone warbles several times. A click and then we hear:

WOMAN'S VOICE [*Filtered, cheerily*]: Hi! You've reached the Armors. Del and I are not in just at the present, but if you leave your name and number — the time and date you called — and, hopefully, a cheerful message, one of us will get back to you just as soon as possible. Don't forget to wait for the ever-lovin' you-know-what, which should be right about—

[*Her recorded message is interrupted by the machine's beep. After the beep.*]

MAN'S VOICE [*Filtered*]: Del? This is Everett. It's Thursday, five forty-eight p.m. Give me a call before you leave for the airport, if you get a chance, okay?

[*Hurrying on from offstage, in a terry robe, drying his hair with a towel, is* ARMOR]

ARMOR [*Getting the phone*]: Hold on, Ev. I'm here. Hold on. Let me turn this thing off. [*Turning off the answering machine*] Ev? Did you get the poop on Dytronix? What's their bid going to be, do we know? ... What? Wait, I've got to take another — hold on. [*Takes a "call waiting"*] Hello? ... Listen, you make one more obscene phone call and I'll have your ass, fuckface! These can be traced, you know. Don't think you're going to get away with this forever! ... That's it. You just keep that foul mouth going. Sooner or later, they're going to close in on you and chop up that Goddamn tongue for dog meat! Bastard! [*Resuming his first call*] Ev? No, no, I'm with you. It was some pervert's been calling here for weeks. I don't care for myself, but it just sickens Mrs. Armor. [*Switching gears*] Now, what do you mean, you haven't got a clue? If Dytronix gets that tank contract and we don't, we're finished, Ev; the company's down the tubes, you know that, don't you? ... Yeah, yeah. Right, right. You find out what you can. I'll try to do the same from Chicago.

> [*He hangs up, a portrait of despondency. A door opens, offstage, then:*]

MYRA'S VOICE [*Offstage*]: Del? Honey, I'm home!

> [*A beat, then* MYRA *enters. Wearing a smart suit, topped by the floral scarf and carrying the same shopping bag established in the previous scene,* MYRA *is now very much the proper housewife. Exchanging air kisses:*]

Darling.

ARMOR: Sweetheart.

MYRA: Sorry I'm late. I was tied up for awhile.

ARMOR: No problem.

MYRA [*Getting her suitcase*]: Any calls?

ARMOR: Uh uh.

MYRA [*Amused*]: My God, you're a terrible liar.

ARMOR: It was another one of those.

MYRA: That guy?

[ARMOR *nods*]

Well, now, why wouldn't you tell me that?

ARMOR: What's the point in upsetting you? I hate for you to even have to use the phone after he's contaminated it. I'll just never understand how the same Lord who created you ever came up with that animal.

MYRA: I love that you want to protect me, darling.

ARMOR: America and you, that's all I care about. And I put that in alphabetical order.

MYRA [*Begins packing*]: Well, we're going to have a whole day away from any kind of annoying calls. A whole day away from everything. Any preference in my undies? Black? Red? Or none?

[ARMOR *smiles weakly*]

Del? You alright? Have you packed, sweetie?

ARMOR: No. Not yet.

MYRA: You said you'd be ready. Now, that's naughty. I really ought to spank you, you know. [*Smiles*] Or do you want to wait until we get to Chicago? [*A beat*] Gosh, I love that town. We've had some wonderful times there, haven't we?

ARMOR [*Starting to dress*]: I guess, yeah.

MYRA [*Pouting*]: You guess? Del, you courted me there. We first — you-know-what — there. Your wife killed herself when she found out about us there. And you *guess*?

ARMOR: Sorry, sweetheart. My mind is just in a whole other place.

MYRA [*Going to him*]: Is there room for two there? What is it, precious? What's troubling you? You know we can't hide anything from each other.

ARMOR: I didn't want to go into it.

MYRA: Into what?

ARMOR [*A beat, then*]: What did you do today, Myra?

MYRA [*Keeping her cool*]: Me? Why do you ask?

ARMOR: Let me answer that for you. You brightened the corner wherever you were. Wherever you went, whatever you did, people felt just that little bit higher for having been with you.

MYRA: A girl does her best.

ARMOR: You want to know what I did today? You want to know how your husband brightened a few lives? He laid off another five thousand employees at the company.

MYRA: Del! Oh, poor darling.

ARMOR: That makes over twenty thousand workers Loyal Armaments has had to let go since the first of the year. Some of the very best makers of hand grenades, of concussive shells and anti-personnel mines. Good, decent people who wouldn't hurt a fly. Today, I fired everybody who manufactures our chemical weapons and gasses. There were tears in their eyes when I told them.

MYRA: Darling, I know things are rough right now ...

ARMOR: Rough? They're disastrous. First, the Wall coming down. Then, Russia starting to fall apart. It's getting so I'm afraid to pick up a newspaper. My God, disarmament, for God's sake! Not just talk. Actual disarmament. I'm all for world peace, but why in *my* time? [*In physical distress*] Where are those pills Dr. Billings prescribed for me?

MYRA: You know you're only supposed to take those if you don't want to feel well.

ARMOR: Myra, Myra! [*Searching for the pills*] I'm going to pieces, Mommy. I really am. [*He finds the pills*]

MYRA: You're doing no such thing.

ARMOR [*Pathetically*]: I love our lifestyle. I like getting the Fruit-of-the-Month from King Hussein. I don't want to have to cut back.

MYRA: We're not going to, I promise you.

ARMOR: But the business gets worse and worse. You've been more than generous, you've been fantastic, but, honey, we can't go on living off the money from your inheritance.

MYRA: Del, what's the first line of the speech you're going to give tomorrow night?

ARMOR: What?

MYRA: How are you starting your speech in Chicago, do you remember?

ARMOR: "Dear Fellow Defense Contractors?"

MYRA: Keep going.

ARMOR: "Dear Fellow Defense Contractors — as we enter this new decade, as we advance on the unknown, let me assure you that we have nothing to fear but the absence of fear itself."

MYRA: "The *absence* of fear itself." Listen to your own words, Del. Stop looking at the sunny side. Things are going to get worse. You've got to have faith.

ARMOR: I try. Nobody prays harder for that than I do.

MYRA: Put those prayers into action, sweetie! Start now! Start today! Beat out Dytronix on that tank contract!

ARMOR [*Frustrated*]: We don't know what their bid is! I don't know how low to go!

MYRA: You can do it. Nobody knows how to be lower than you do.

ARMOR: Thanks, darling. [*A deep sigh*] It might just be I'm getting too old for all this.

MYRA: Oh, pish. You're as vital and strong as you were the first time we met. Remember?

ARMOR [*Recalling*]: "Oh, Stewardess? I wonder if you could bring me a pillow and a blanket, when you have a chance?"

MYRA [*Playing along*]: "Certainly. Is there anything else I can do for you, Mr. Armor?"

ARMOR: That was fate, you know. Pure fate that sent you to me when I pressed that button.

MYRA: You *still* know how to press the right buttons. [*So saying, she tugs at one end of his robe belt*]

ARMOR [*His confidence restored*]: I'm going to get that contract!

MYRA: All right!

ARMOR: I'm going to build that tank!

MYRA: You betcha!

ARMOR: With the longest cannon you ever saw!

MYRA: The longest and the biggest!

> [*Their mutual arousal is cut short by an offstage car horn*]

MYRA: The car.

ARMOR: Wait! Before we go? Just a kiss from your grateful puppy?

MYRA: You got it.

> [*She steps out of her heels.* ARMOR *gets to his knees and begins to kiss her toes. As he does, she slowly encircles his neck with her scarf, elegantly, momentarily, strangling him. The lights go down*]

Scene 7 — A golf Course

In the darkness, we hear:

A MAN'S VOICE [*Offstage, filtered*]: Next on the first tee on the Gerald Ford Course, Mr. Armor and General Graves, please. Mr. Armor and General Graves. Eight minute call for Senator Diehl, Colonel Coffin, Judge Bench and Admiral Bragg.

> [*Lights up, on the first hole of: A Golf Course. There is a small bench, a ball washer/shoe scraper and white markers to indicate the men's tee. GRAVES, in colorful golf clothes, is warming up, using his driver to flex his upper body, doing knee bends, etc. He checks his watch, looks out front over the "fairway" then takes a few practice swings. A beat, then ARMOR appears, golf club in hand, and dressed to play. Obviously rushed, his shoes are untied*]

ARMOR: Sorry, Sherm.

GRAVES: No problem, Del. We've got a couple of foursomes ahead of us. We're probably going to want to play through.

ARMOR [*Sitting, tying his shoes*]: Traffic was murder. It was like trying to get out of Kuwait City during the turkey shoot.

GRAVES: I came by chopper. Thanks to you.

ARMOR: That's why the company's got 'em.

GRAVES: It's a damn fine machine.

ARMOR: I keep telling you, any time you have the need for one, carte blanche is the name of the game.

GRAVES: I thank you very much, Del. Thank you loud and clear.

ARMOR [*Looking out at the fairway*]: What're they, *all* in the woods?

GRAVES: I'm in no hurry, if you're not.

ARMOR: No, no, I'm fine. That's an awfully good-looking stick you've got there.

GRAVES: Matsui. Japanese.

ARMOR: Naturally. May I?

   [GRAVES *hands him the club*]

Graphite, of course. [*After a few practise swings*] Light as a feather.

GRAVES: They wrote the book.

ARMOR: Really. What the hell do they know that we don't?

GRAVES: How to be us.

ARMOR: I guess. Right. [*Returning the club*] It's terrific.

GRAVES: They were giving them out at the Hiroshima Open.

ARMOR: I tried like hell to get over for that.

GRAVES: It was outstanding. Of course, the first hole is a real son-of-a-bitch.

[*Both men laugh*]

ARMOR [*Squinting out at the fairway*]: We may be out here longer than it took you to wrap up the Iraqi caper.

GRAVES: Well, we had the lights all the way on that one.

ARMOR: You're probably tired of hearing it, Sherm, but that was some kind of show you boys put on over there.

GRAVES: It was long overdue, that's for sure. I'll tell you when war is really hell, my friend. When they don't let you win one. It was a great relief to finally be turned loose. To do our job without being told how to do it and to not have to answer to anyone about the way we did it. Incentivized all of us in the military. Restored our pride. Our stature. Gave us back our dignity.

ARMOR [*A beat*]: Were you serious the other day? When you told Oprah Winfrey you might be retiring?

GRAVES: I was part of a team that helped send a third rate power back to the Flintstones. I always wanted to end on a high note. It's time to hang up the old stars.

ARMOR: Have you thought about what's next?

GRAVES: I'm not even thinking about thinking about it yet. I want to do some painting. Travel. Visit some parts of the world I've only seen through a bomb sight. I might do some writing. Or maybe a lecture tour, one victory lap around the country, so to speak. My biggest problem right now is whether to go with CAA or the William Morris Agency.

ARMOR: Sherm, are you aware how many of our presidents were men who had illustrious military careers?

GRAVES [*Off-handedly*]: Never given it that much thought.

ARMOR: Something like seven or eight.

GRAVES: Ten.

ARMOR: Say the word, and we can make it eleven.

GRAVES: Whoa, there. Steady, Del.

ARMOR: I've put together a committee, Sherm. Wait. Hear me out. It's very informal. Just a dozen of us so far. We've chipped in a little seed money to get a few polls, a few surveys going, set up a staff to study a variety of positions on issues we think you might consider feeling strongly about.

GRAVES: There are better men for the job, Del. We both know that.

ARMOR: No offense, Sherm, but the people don't always want the better man. I can name you any number of presidents we put on a pedestal so we didn't have to look down on them. Continue the tradition of Washington and Grant and Eisenhower, Sherm. Let us move you into Pennsylvania Avenue.

GRAVES [*Laughs*]: At ease, Del. You're moving awful fast for me.

ARMOR [*A beat*]: Just one more word on the subject? If you should decide to run? As I said, we've put some money together to get the presidential ball rolling, but we could build a really enormous war chest for you if Loyal Armaments were to land the new tank contract the Pentagon's getting ready to put out.

GRAVES: For the sake of our friendship, Del, don't make me hear something that I might have to testify about somewhere down the line that I didn't.

ARMOR: Sherm, you must believe me when I tell you I would rather cut my company's profits in half for a month rather than take a chance on jeopardizing our relationship. Just hear me out, then you do what's fair. All I want you to give me is a chief executive-type decision.

GRAVES [*Feeling just the little bit more presidential*]: What is it?

ARMOR: I don't have to tell you about Loyal Armaments. We started out in my ex-father-in-law's garage. Our real break was Korea. That was our first government contract. [*Fondly*] We brewed our own napalm. My late wife helped with the cooking. Even the kids joined in, after school. We never looked back after that. Ammo, rockets, land mines, booby-trapped soft toys. Loyal was anywhere you looked in Laos, in Cambodia, in Vietnam. It was Loyal that helped United States Marines liberate American students from Cuban construction workers in Grenada. When our air force destroyed the neighborhoods of Panama City to free the people of their homes under Noriega, they did it with Loyal missiles. I don't have to tell you the job we did during "Desert Storm," where the best stuff on both sides was ours. Loyal has served everywhere that you have, Sherm. Everywhere in the world that we have kicked ass for God and country.

GRAVES: For which I say, amen.

ARMOR: Everyone in the defense community wants that tank contract, Sherm. But Loyal's got the goods. We can fill the bill.

GRAVES: Then there's every chance that you might get it.

ARMOR: We've spent over two billion in research on this project, Sherm. That's a lot of money just to buy a chance.

GRAVES: There's no way to go around the procedure. You can't outflank fairness.

ARMOR: We consider our only real competition is Dytronix.

GRAVES: I'm not going to ask you how you know that.

ARMOR: We've learned that Dytronix is going to submit a bid significantly lower than ours and yet their profit will still be the standard ten times more than it ought to be.

GRAVES: Well, we'd be delighted if you can lowball them, of course. Any weapon we can save the taxpayer money on allows us to buy just that many more weapons.

ARMOR: There's only one way we can do that. We know that Dytronix's bid is either four or five billion less than our's, but we can't be certain. We've tried infiltrating them, but it's impossible. Their security is impenetrable.

GRAVES: You'll get no criticism from me about that sort of vigilance. As far as I'm concerned, when it comes to the nation's security, I find even paranoia to be a half measure.

ARMOR: I agree, absolutely. Happily, for my purposes, a copy of their bid can be found inside the Pentagon, where security is nowhere near as tight.

GRAVES: You can hardly expect a sense of duty to be a match for free enterprise.

ARMOR: All we need to know is whether to bid four or five billion less, Sherm. We need nothing more than that. Just four or five. Just one little number and it makes all the difference in the world as to whether or not Loyal goes on arming America into the next century — and whether or not this country has the golden opportunity of being led by a man with the common touch and strength of a Truman; the charisma of a Kennedy — [*Building*] the combined power of both Roosevelts; the accessibility, and yet the lonely, splendid majesty of an Abraham Lincoln.

GRAVES [*Looking down the fairway*]: I think we can play now. [*Teeing his ball*] Not a soul out there. No chance of hitting anybody.

ARMOR: Right.

[GRAVES *gets ready to swing, then calls out:*]

GRAVES: Fore!

ARMOR [*Looking out at the fairway, confused*]: Fore?

GRAVES [*For* ARMOR's *benefit*]: Fore.

[ARMOR, *getting the message, breaks into a broad smile. As* GRAVES *reaches the top of his backswing: Blackout*]

Scene 8 — An Industrial Dump Site

A pair of headlights appear, giving the impression of a an oncoming car parking offstage. The headlights are turned off. The engine is killed. The lights of a second car approach. It parks offstage on the opposite side of the first car and its headlights go off. A car phone warbles once. Then:

GRAVES [*Voice over; flatly, filtered*]: You smile the song begins, you speak and I hear violins.

KEENE [*Voice over; the same*]: It's magic.

GRAVES [*Voice over; a beat*]: You're certain you weren't followed?

KEENE [*Voice over*]: Reasonably. My car or yours? How do we play it?

GRAVES [*Voice over*]: Either one could be bugged.

KEENE [*Voice over*]: As well as these phones.

GRAVES [*Voice over*]: Right!

> [*A beat, then the offstage car doors open and close.* CONGRESSWOMAN KEENE *enters from one side. From the other, in uniform,* GRAVES *enters, three stars on the epaulets of his officer's trench coat. They go to each other, looking about, making sure they*

are not being observed. When they are close:]

GRAVES: Congresswoman.

KEENE: General.

GRAVES: Good of you to meet me at this hour and in this not terribly attractive setting.

KEENE: Nothing is too unattractive when it comes to national security, sir.

GRAVES: My very credo.

KEENE: And how may I help you?

GRAVES: I don't know if you're aware that I may soon be retiring.

KEENE: As a matter of fact, I saw you announce it on "Donahue."

GRAVES: My fifteen minutes to be a celebrity, I suppose.

KEENE: You've earned it, sir. The ticker tape *and* the video tape.

GRAVES: I simply did my duty. I had no idea it would turn out to be as heroic as it did.

KEENE: There's some talk that you may run for office. One that might just be Oval in nature?

GRAVES: The subject has been semi-broached.

KEENE: Does that possibility have anything to do with wanting to see me? You're not shopping around for someone for second place on the ticket?

GRAVES: I am not here to ask you to be my running mate, no. Even though I have the highest regard for the women I spent so much time in the sand with. I'm not one of those who believe that a woman's place is in the field kitchen. That is not why I asked you here tonight.

> [*To avoid a pair of oncoming headlights, they duck momentarily behind some leaking oil drums marked "Toxic." Reappearing:*]

Whatever's next for me, Congresswoman, I want to be sure, I need to be absolutely certain, that I'm leaving a spotless record behind.

KEENE: And what might possibly prevent that, sir?

GRAVES: I know that you are preparing to subpoena me to come before your committee.

KEENE: And do you have any idea what it is I want you to tell us?

GRAVES: I only know that you and I are looking for two different kinds of headlines. Such an appearance could prove most harmful to me at this particular juncture in time. I'd like to make you a proposal.

KEENE: You've got a nice, full moon to do it under.

GRAVES: I'm offering to tell you something you do not know in exchange for not telling everyone whatever it is that you do. Is that acceptable to you?

KEENE: I'll know that only after I know what I now don't.

GRAVES: No guarantees beforehand?

KEENE: Sweep me off my feet, General.

GRAVES: You are familiar with my role in the development of the B-3 bomber?

KEENE: I know that you acted as the Pentagon liaison during the construction of the B-3 at the Dytronix Industries plant in Placenta, California.

GRAVES: Precisely. But I'm afraid that although Dytronix was awarded the half trillion dollar contract to build the bomber, that decision was, unfortunately, based on test results that were falsified. Fraudulent.

KEENE: The tests were faked?

GRAVES: The tests themselves were not. The test results were.

KEENE: This charge is staggering in its implications.

GRAVES [*Producing a document from his attache case*]: I've

prepared a true account of the event. The most pertinent passages relate to a simulated bombing run we ran, to check out the efficiency of the B-3's delivery system over enemy targets.

KEENE: Live bombs were used, as indicated? That much is true?

GRAVES: In imaginary situations, there is no substitute for reality. The target zone was an abandoned quarry, located twenty miles outside of what was formerly the town of Winsock, Oklahoma. Unfortunately, once the onboard computer mistakenly kicked in the plane's heat-seeking device, the result was inevitable.

KEENE [*Horrified, looking at the document*]: Is this true? The plane dropped its payload on a church cookout?

GRAVES: To a computer, when you're hot, you're hot. Heat is heat, whether it's coming from a blast furnace in Baghdad or a Baptist barbecue. In all honesty, it was not entirely the fault of the equipment. I mean, they were asking for it, in a way, with all those briquettes going.

KEENE: General, this is beyond horrendous. This can't be true? The entire town was destroyed? Wiped out?

GRAVES: There was an unfortunate amount of collateral damage, yes.

KEENE: And just how many collateral dead?

GRAVES: As near as we can determine, about twelve hundred.

KEENE: Twelve hundred people died?

GRAVES: As a result of friendly incineration, yes, ma'am. Do we have a deal, Congresswoman? Is what I've told you more important than whatever it is you're hoping to finding out?

KEENE [*A beat*]: Are you familiar with a Mr. Charles Worth, General?

GRAVES: I know the name.

KEENE: Mr. Worth is, among other things, chairman and president of Dytronix Industries, is he not?

GRAVES: He is.

KEENE: And you have been a guest of Mr. Worth's on more than one occasion?

GRAVES: That's how I know the name.

KEENE: Most recently, of course, you visited the home of Mr. Worth when you attended his daughter's wedding several weeks ago.

GRAVES: I dare say just about everyone in Washington did.

KEENE: Indeed. Anyone who ever bought anyone was there.

GRAVES: That's a bit strong, I must —

KEENE [*Cutting in*]: You would have no way of knowing it, General, but on that occasion, Mr. Worth was wearing a special Justice Department device which enabled him to tape a virtual album of governmental abuse.

GRAVES: Are you saying he was wired?

KEENE: Like a Christmas tree, sir.

[*As* GRAVES *reflects on this*]

Every conversation he had on that particular day was recorded. Including one that took place between just the two of you in his greenhouse. Do you happen to recall it? [*She takes an audio cassette from her attache case*] I can play it for you in my car, if you like. It's the one in which he discusses whether you'd like your payment in cash or deposited in a numbered account.

GRAVES: I recall no such conversation.

KEENE: Just a short time later, Mr. Worth, in a private conversation with his wife, boasts that he has a certain general in his pocket. A certain general who will be going to work as a consultant for Dytronix — officially — once he retires from the service. Of course, all this happened before the Loyal people offered you the opportunity to become their "consultant" in the White House. [*A beat; then, re the document*] I thank you for these papers, General. [*Placing it in her case, and producing one of her own*] Turnabout is fair play. [*She hands it to him*]

GRAVES [*Dismayed*]: This is a subpoena.

KEENE: It is.

GRAVES: We had a deal.

KEENE: To talk about a deal.

GRAVES [*Tempting her, hopefully*]: Actually, there will be room for second place on the ticket, I think I can promise you that.

KEENE: I'll just wait until there's room at the top. Goodnight, sir. And do be careful. This is a very rough neighborhood.

> [*As she leaves* GRAVES, *a lot sadder and no wiser at all: Lights fade out*]

Scene 9 — A Rectory

A tea service is set up on a small table. LITTLE, *in black suit and dog collar, is fiddling with the tape deck that is emitting organ music. Seated on a chair, is* KEENE.

LITTLE: It's not too loud? You don't find this intrusive?

KEENE: I find it very comforting.

LITTLE: It is, isn't it? I'm addicted to the organ. To me, it transcends music. I've always thought of it as the sound of eternity.

KEENE: I suppose it is, yes, in a way.

LITTLE [*Crossing to the tea things*]: And now, something in the key of "T," perhaps?

KEENE: Lovely.

LITTLE [*Pouring*]: Will you take lemon or milk?

KEENE: I'll have it straight, please.

LITTLE: Just as it comes. [*Finishes pouring*] And come it has. [*He hands her her cup*]

KEENE: Thank you.

LITTLE [*Pouring for himself*]: Nothing like a cup of tea is there, to get you through whatever's next?

KEENE: And God knows there's always something that is.

LITTLE: Of that, we can be certain. There are those times when life seems an exam we're taking and the hall bell is broken. [*Offering the pastry tray*] Can I tempt you?

KEENE: Thank you, no.

LITTLE: Are you sure? My Mrs. Brady makes them for me. Fiendishly good. The woman's buns will be the death of me yet. [*Sits, raises his teacup to her in a toast*] Bottoms up. [*A slight chuckle, a sip of his tea, and then*] Before you say anything, you must believe me when I tell you I was about to telephone you not half a second before your own call came.

KEENE: Oh?

LITTLE: I only just learned that you're scheduled to read the speech I've been delivering on my national tour into the Congressional Record. I can't tell you what an action such as yours means to me. Not just in the matter of arousing contributors. The entire effort of my battered women's foundation is given a huge thrust when you allow yourself to be identified as one of my supporters.

KEENE: I felt your words merited the praise that that

recognition symbolizes.

LITTLE: The praise belongs to those distressed souls, those battered women, whose numbers are legion, who are forced to endure the pain and terror that the last vestige of beast in man metes out to them. All I do is remain faithful to my calling. [*Re her tea cup*] Can I top that up a bit for you?

KEENE: Thank you. [*As he does:*] On the subject of women with problems — [*She hesitates*]

LITTLE: Yes?

KEENE: Perhaps you can help me.

LITTLE: In any way that I can, you know that.

KEENE: I've been contacted lately by a number of my constituents. Three different women. Neither knows any of the others, but each of them is going through the same, truly nightmarish experience.

LITTLE: They're being battered?

KEENE: In a manner of speaking. [*A beat*] They're being telephoned.

LITTLE: Oh?

KEENE: It's a form of audio abuse. Of telephonic torment. Of A.T. and T. S and M.

LITTLE: Horrible.

KEENE: Representative Howell. Of New Jersey?

LITTLE: I know the name.

KEENE: Four women from her district have all reported the same experience. The same man. The same routines. He's dialing homes in Maine, Vermont, New Hampshire. He finishes one, hangs up, then calls another. He's got the fastest finger in the northeast.

LITTLE: You're sure, they're sure, it's the same man?

KEENE: We've compared notes. There's no question about it.

LITTLE: He says the same thing to each of them.

KEENE: To each of us.

LITTLE: He's called you, as well?

KEENE: Oh, yes. I got what the women refer to as a — may I speak freely?

LITTLE: I daresay I've heard it all by now. There are only so many variations on the theme.

KEENE: What they call a conference, or gang bang call. He's not just one of your common, garden variety heavy breathers. Not this sicko. He's got dozens of scenarios, but for this one he's apparently pre-recorded six or seven other male voices, all his own, one can only hope. If you don't hang up or the man of the house doesn't come on and threaten to punch his lights out, the caller then hits what must be the foreplay button on his tape recorder, and the next thing you know, there are half dozen guys inside your ear making you feel, as he puts it, as though you're spread-eagled atop a pool table, with each of them sinking their shots in your corner pocket. [*A beat*] I'm sorry. Is this more than you want to hear?

LITTLE: Certainly a bit more than I expected.

KEENE: The feeling is he's even happier if the woman is out. That way there's always the chance that one of the children might pick it up. He has a separate repertoire for the kids. Nursery rhymes. Limericks.

LITTLE: Oh, dear.

KEENE: The kind where the first line ends with words like "rocksucker."

LITTLE: Dear, dear, dear. [*Crossing to the tape deck*] This hardly seems appropriate. [*He turns off the music. Wiping his brow:*] The idea of a child playing something like that over and over and over and over.

KEENE: Must make his mouth water. But, then, I think most everything must make him a little damp.

LITTLE: Have you been to the police? Has anyone?

KEENE: We're dealing with a pro. He knows just when to get off. No pun intended.

LITTLE: Sorry?

KEENE: He'll speak just so long and not a second longer. He knows when to hang up so he can't be traced to his number. Obviously, he times each call. He also seems to travel from time to time. Being out of town so much, not having a set pattern, makes it even more difficult to know where and when he's going to pop up. He must know that, of course.

LITTLE: I would say.

KEENE: The police tell me they've worked out a plan; some sort of scheme they think may expose him. They say that, barring the possibility of his voluntary surrender and subsequent confession, they should be able to locate and arrest him inside three or four more calls — if he chooses to make anymore.

LITTLE: Well, that certainly sets my prayer agenda for awhile.

KEENE [*Agreeing*]: Mmm.

LITTLE: And in which way can I be of help?

KEENE: I don't know if you're familiar with the bill I'm trying to get through the House. My bill on abortion.

LITTLE: I am. And, quite frankly, I find it just that.

KEENE: You can imagine my amazement, then — and my delight — when my press people showed me this release.

[*She hands him a page of paper. He reads it, a frown forming*]

LITTLE: Where did this come from?

KEENE: My press office, as I said.

LITTLE: By what authority?

KEENE: My own, actually.

LITTLE: This hasn't gone out on the wire, has it? It hasn't been printed anywhere?

KEENE: No, no. We want to run your picture with it, if you have a favorite you'd like to give me.

LITTLE: But this is outrageous. You may not say that I support your bill on abortion, when you know I've stated over and over that I wish that bill would die.

KEENE: Consistency is the mark of a small mind, is it not?

LITTLE: The position of the church —

KEENE [*Cutting in*]: Ah, but there are an endless number of positions, aren't there? And I'm the one you really want to get behind, aren't I? The one it would be much better to push?

LITTLE [*Perplexed*]: You simply must understand.

KEENE: Oh, but I do. Everything. And you must remain faithful to your calling. [*Silence a moment. She eyes the pastry tray*] They are deadly, aren't they? Mrs. Brady's buns. [*Taking a bite of one*] So puffy and firm. I bet they melt in your mouth. [*As she refills his teacup:*] This is going to be a wonderful association. This is just the beginning.

LITTLE: But we have diametrically opposite ideas on just about everything. We are worlds apart on foreign policy, on censorship, on sex education. I will lose my entire credibility.

KEENE: Not to those who are programmed to accept whatever you say. You'll get a copy of whatever statements my staff decides you're to deliver. And deliver it you will. [*Reminding him*] Just as it comes. Well — [*Raising her cup*] Bottoms up. Huge thrust. Addicted to the organ, and all that.

> [*She drinks. He doesn't. Gathering her attache case:*]

Glad to have you on board, sir.

> [LITTLE *is too defeated to respond*]

My office will arrange some photo opportunities and a few speaking engagements. It'll take a lot of coordination. We'll have to work it all out with my young women. [*Starts to leave, stops for one last thought*] But don't call us. We'll call you.

[*And she exits, leaving him in ruins. Lights fade*]

POWER FAILURE

Scene 10 — Death Row

WILL's *prison cell on death row. A red phone has been installed.* WILL, *alone, sits reading a book, titled:* "'Will's Way,' by B. J. Coyne." *A highlighter in hand,* WILL *is highly disturbed by the book's contents.*

WILL: Son-of-a-bitch! [*He turns the page, is further angered by what he reads. Making swift, emphatic strokes with his highlighter:*] Jesus!

[LITTLE *enters, bible in hand*]

LITTLE: Good morning, Will.

[WILL *ignores him, continues to scribble feverishly*]

LITTLE [*Patiently*]: Will? I said good morning.

WILL: Oh, really? You and I must be in two completely different mornings. [*He highlights a page, wildly, trying to obliterate the words; then, he rips the page out of the book and crumples it*] Have you read this?

LITTLE [*Lifting his bible slightly*]: You have your book, I have mine.

WILL: And I'm guilty in both of them, right? [*Nods at bible*] You think he was crucified? You know how many times she sat in that same chair you're in right now?

190

You know how many times she said, "This book'll do it for you, Will"? "This book is your ticket back to life." [*Recalling*] "There's not a fiber in my private or professional being that doesn't believe in your complete innocence." She said that. That's exactly what she said. Word for word. Lie for lie.

LITTLE: Will. There is so little time.

WILL: You think I didn't know that before you got here? Time! God, the hours I wasted spilling my guts for her, talking my heart out. Hours and hours. I could have been — I don't know — doing something, anything. Maybe they'd have let me weave a basket. Or make a license plate. Yeah, that'd be good. A license plate. Personalized. [*Visualizing it*] "CORPSE." Wouldn't it be beautiful? It winds up on some car on the outside. And the guy's driving along, not paying too much attention, and he's going just a little too fast. And then she steps off the curb. Little Miss Not-A-Fucking-Fiber gets to the middle of the street, but she don't see my plates coming because she's too busy thinking how to stick it to me and Wham! She gets it! [*He pounds a fist into a palm. Then, quickly*] Not hard! No! She's just knocked down. [*A gentler fist into his palm*] His bumper catches right in the knees, just enough to snap 'em. She hits the street and he keeps moving forward. He don't even know. He was looking at the stereo, maybe making a phone call.

LITTLE: Will.

WILL: Her hair's caught in his bumper and he about

scalps her as she's dragged along under the car.

LITTLE: You have only moments.

WILL: She's having the hide ripped off her back, only she can't scream, 'cause she's got a mouth full of crankcase oil. [*A beat*] Why the hell they put that phone in here? It's never going to ring. You read what the governor said.

LITTLE: There is always a chance.

WILL: If she had any doubts at all, the book removed them. This God damn book!

LITTLE: The governor is a woman of some mercy. We have seen that in her.

WILL: If I'm gone when she calls, take a message.

LITTLE: I'd like to give you some comfort, Will; help you, if you'll let me.

WILL: Like she did? [*Re book*]: You don't have to peek at the end to see who did it. Uh uh. No, sir. First page. First word. [*Reads it*] "Guilty." Beautiful, huh? [*Reads on*] "He greets you with a look that says, 'I've lost the girl I took to the prom and the two daughters she bore me. Help share my grief before it crushes me.' But the only word that occurs comes to the mind and not the heart. And that word is 'guilty.'" Sucked me in, that's what she did. She just sucked me in, you know what I'm saying?

LITTLE: Yes.

WILL: Sat right there and gave me a royal screwing. [*Beat*] You know how long it's been since I've been with a woman? And then, in she comes and she sits where you're sitting, day after day, half the time with her skirt up over her knees. Like just 'cause I'm in here, I forgot what a woman's legs lead to.

[LITTLE *seeks escape by looking into his bible*]

So I close my eyes to block that out, but after she leaves, there's still the sound of her voice. When a man talks, it's just talk. When a woman talks, I hear her with my whole body. Just remembering her voice was enough to give me ideas there was no way I could follow through where they were taking me. [*A beat*] Can I ask you to do something?

LITTLE: I would like to.

WILL: Would you call her?

LITTLE: Call her?

WILL: After. Or before. Or during, I don't care, it don't matter. Give her a message for me. Tell her I said it's okay. Tell her I understand. She did what she had to do. Nobody's any different that way, are we?

LITTLE: That will please her, Will.

WILL: You think so? I'm really doing it more for me

than for her. If I forgive her, maybe somebody'll forgive me.

LITTLE: We all deserve forgiveness. It remains only to admit the act for which we require forgiveness in order to petition for it.

WILL: You got a watch?

LITTLE: I do.

WILL: I don't want to know the time.

LITTLE: I understand.

WILL: But is it, yet?

LITTLE [*Checking his watch*]: Not quite.

[*Silence a moment, then*]

WILL [*Re phone*]: You suppose the governor's sitting by her phone, at the other end?

LITTLE: That is my prayer, Will.

WILL [*A beat*]: Jesus, I hope they don't get Dustin Hoffman.

LITTLE: Pardon?

WILL: To play me. If there's a movie. That would be the last kick in the ass. He's always playing weirdos.

Guys in dresses. Tom Cruise's dumb brother. What a way to be remembered. [*Scans book*] She got where she got on her own, I'll give her that. But she never got the real story. Chalk one up for me. [*He puts his forefinger to his tongue and strokes the air before him. A beat, then*] You know why I did it, don't you? Did what I really did that I said was a dream?

LITTLE: No, Will, I don't.

WILL: This is between us.

LITTLE: Of course.

WILL: You don't write books?

LITTLE: What you say will go no farther.

WILL [*Another beat, then*]: It was because of him.

LITTLE: Him?

WILL: The guy.

LITTLE: There was another man?

WILL: There was. Yeah.

LITTLE: Your wife was unfaithful?

[WILL *shakes his head*]

Did you know him?

WILL: Only from the calls.

LITTLE: The calls?

WILL: The calls she got from him on the phone. On the sly. She didn't know I listened on the extension. I never heard his name. I guess that was part of the deal. She'd get on the horn with this guy and you can't believe the filth I heard. Once, it was like a party. She took him on and maybe half a dozen of his friends from a pool hall, all saying what they were going to do to her. This is my wife we're talking about, you understand. This is not some 900 number where you call up and they come in your ear for two dollars a minute.

LITTLE: I understand.

WILL: This is my wife. The mother of my girls. I never went anywhere, people wanted to take them home with them, that's the kind of beautiful they were. And this creep, out of the blue, he calls and when he can't talk to her, he leaves messages for my kids. I come home and my little girls are playing these tapes. As much as you've heard in all your days, you never heard stuff like this. And these are babies. Babies! [*A beat*] I had to kill 'em to save 'em. I killed 'em to take 'em out of this terrible world. How could I let them stay here? A world where children have their minds raped? Where they see their own father kill their own mother? How could I ever face them again after that? [*A beat, then*] Thank you, Father.

LITTLE: No!

WILL: Thank you for being here when I said it.

[*A metal door clangs open offstage*]

Time for my shot.

LITTLE [*Moving toward him*]: Will.

WILL: Nobody's coming with me.

LITTLE: Forgive me, Will.

WILL: Huh?

LITTLE: I didn't mean it. I couldn't help it either.

WILL: Help what?

LITTLE: Each living thing adds to the misery of another. None of us is innocent. Each unkind act creates a circuitry of its own, a grid based on the evil we call desire, against which we are all helpless. There is purity only in that life we know before we ever know it. Only there, in mother's warm, wet womb.

[WILL *is arrested by the sound of* LITTLE's *voice*]

WILL: Say something for me, would you?

LITTLE: Say something?

WILL: Anything.

LITTLE [*Opening his bible*]: Malachi. Chapter Two. "Behold I will corrupt your seed, and spread dung upon your faces." [*Realizing the inappropriateness of his selection, he turns to another page, and reads*] "If any man have ears to hear, let him hear."

WILL: Your voice ...

LITTLE: Forgive me, Will.

> [*Before* WILL *can place it, he is distracted by the offstage sound of the gurney being wheeled by*]

WILL: There goes the gurney. [*A beat*] I thought I'd be more scared. Maybe 'cause I'm going to see my girls again. And all that bad stuff's behind us, huh?

LITTLE: The denial's behind you. That's why you've shed your fear. We need to answer for our sins, Will. Each of us. The worst of all punishments is to go unpunished. To be sentenced to a never-ending expectation of discovery. And to dread that it will never come, that we will never know the pain we feel we have surely earned.

> [*The cell door opens.* WILL *starts for it*]

Let me come with you.

WILL [*Stops, turns*]: What?

LITTLE: Let me come with you.

WILL [*Testing him*]: Let me come with you — Marilyn.

LITTLE [*Beat*]: Let me come with you, Marilyn.

> [*A long moment, as* WILL *tries hard to remember. Putting it all together, he looks at* LITTLE *with horror.* LITTLE *cannot face him.* WILL, *numbed by what he now knows has gone before, and what lies in the moments ahead, exits into the shadows.* LITTLE, *left alone with his guilt and his shame, understands that there is only one action he can take. Putting his bible aside, he places his handkerchief over the red phone's receiver. Then, lifting the receiver to his ear, he begins to dial. And, for the last time: The lights fade out*]

CITY OF ANGELS

Book by Larry Gelbart
Lyrics by David Zippel

"There's a miracle on Broadway, an *American* musical, with American wisecracks and an original American script. . . It's smart, swinging, sexy and funny. Wit is all over the stage."

—Jack Kroll, *Newsweek*

"Larry Gelbart's book is so brilliantly original, so chills-up-your-spine inventive. . . The jokes snap, the dialogue crackles, the story pops. . . *Angels* put me on Cloud 9."

—Joel Siegel, ABC-TV

"How long has it been since a musical was brought to a halt by riotous jokes? One would have to travel back to the 1960s to find a musical as flat out funny as *City of Angels*."

—Frank Rich, *The New York Times*

"One of the most innovative, brilliant, perfect, breathtaking, entertaining pieces of theatre I have ever seen. The lyrics by David Zippel. . . are bright and diamond hard. . ."

—Liz Smith, *New York Daily News*

cloth ISBN: 1-55783-081-9

APPLAUSE

THE COLLECTED WORKS OF HAROLD CLURMAN

Six Decades of Commentary on Theatre, Dance, Music, Film, Arts, Letters and Politics

edited by Marjorie Loggia and Glenn Young

For six decades, Harold Clurman illuminated our artistic, social and political awareness in thousands of reviews, essays and lectures. In 1930 he began a series of lectures at Steinway Hall that would lead to the creation of the Group Theater. His work appeared indefatigably in *Tomorrow, The New Republic, The London Observer, The New York Times, The Nation, Stagebill, Show, Theatre Arts and New York Magazine.*

This chronological epic offers the most comprehensive view of American theatre seen through the eyes of our most extraordinary critic–the largest collection of criticism by a dramatic critic ever published in the English language.

cloth•ISBN 1-55783-132-7

♥APPLAUSE♥

INSPECTOR
AND OTHER PLAYS
by Nicolai Gogol

English versions by Eric Bentley

Eric Bentley brings to the attention of Gogol's still growing American public not only a new version of *Inspector*, but three other dramatic works: *The Marriage, Gamblers* and *A Madman's Diary*, the last-named being Bentley's dramatization of a famous Gogol story.

In a critical Preface, Bentley finds all four works to be a Gogolian treatment of love—or lack of love—and by the same token, thoroughly original works of dramatic art.

At the back of the book comes a bonus in the shape of a piece on *Gamblers* by the eminent Polish critic Jan Kott.

A chronology and guide to further reading are also provided.

ISBN: 0-936839-12-0

☙APPLAUSE❧

THE MADMAN AND THE NUN and THE CRAZY LOCOMOTIVE

THREE PLAYS (including THE WATER HEN)

by Stanislaw Ignacy Witkiewicz

Edited, translated and with an introduction by Daniel Gerould and C. S. Durer

Foreword by Jan Kott

"It is high time that this major playwright should become better known in the English-speaking world."
—Martin Esslin

STARTLING discontinuities and surprises erupt throughout these avant-garde landscapes by Poland's outstanding modern dramatist. A decadent poet rebels against society's repressive tyranny through suicide and last minute resurrection in *Madman and the Nun*. A band of degenerate criminals and artists in *The Crazy Locomotive* commandeer an engine and seek to bring about God's judgment by racing at apocalyptic speeds into an oncoming passenger train. Painter, photographer, novelist, philosopher, expert on drugs, Witkiewicz exemplifies in these dramas his mastery of a new art of the theatre.

ISBN: 0-936839-83-X

ON THE OPEN ROAD

by **Steve Tesich**

Set in a landscape stripped bare by civil war, two "independents," Al and Angel, forge an alliance of convenience in order to buy their way into the land of the free, the one safe haven in an otherwise lawless landscape. Hiding from marauding armies, they travel the country, gathering great art treasures from crumbling museums. But with the border to fredom in sight, they're captured by forces from the new coalition government. They can still buy thier freedom—if they agree to do one little job for the government.

Steve Tesich has also written the screenplays for *Four Friends*, *The World According to Garp*, *Eleni* and *Breaking Away*, for which he recieved an Oscar.

ISBN: 1-55783-134-3

❁ **APPLAUSE** ❁

A FUNNY THING HAPPENED ON THE WAY TO THE FORUM

Book by Burt Shevelove and Larry Gelbart

Music and Lyrics by Stephen Sondheim

"It is without doubt the most intellectual of all our musical books. . . of all the books ever written, *Forum's* is the least likely to date."

—Martin Gottfried, *Broadway Musicals*

"A good, clean, dirty show! Bring back the belly laughs!"

—*Time*

"It's funny, true nonsense! A merry good time!"

—Walter Kerr, *New York Herald Tribune*

cloth ISBN: 1-55783-063-0

♥APPLAUSE♥

DAVID MERRICK:
THE ABOMINABLE SHOWMAN
THE UNAUTHORIZED BIOGRAPHY
by Howard Kissel

"One of the most magical biographies of the theatre I have ever read. . . Kissel has pulled back the curtain on a fallible, mortal and very complicated man."

—Carol Channing

"Fascinating. . . This rich, anecdote-filled tale is good, dirty fun."

—*Newsweek*

"No theatre buff will want to miss this strong biography."

—*Publishers Weekly*

"Just the ticket for theatre fans."

—*Associated Press*

ISBN: 1-55783-172-6

APPLAUSE

OTHER PEOPLE'S MONEY